Next Stop,
CORNER
OFFICE

YAHOO! hotjobs®

Next Stop, CORNER OFFICE

SUCCESS STRATEGIES FOR
MANAGERS & EXECUTIVES

DAN FINNIGAN AND MARC KARASU

STERLING PUBLISHING
New York

Published by Sterling Publishing Co., Inc.
387 Park Avenue South, New York, NY 10016

Distributed in Canada by Sterling Publishing
c/o Canadian Manda Group, 165 Dufferin Street
Toronto, Ontario M6K 3H6

Distributed in Great Britain by Chrysalis Books Group PLC
The Chrysalis Building, Bramley Road, London W10 6SP, England

Distributed in Australia by Capricorn Link (Australia) Pty. Ltd.
P.O. Box 704, Windsor, NSW 2756, Australia

Library of Congress Cataloging-in-Publication Data available upon request

ISBN 1-4027-2827-1

Printed in the United States of America

10 9 8 7 6 5 4 3 2 1

For information about custom editions, special sales, premium and corporate purchases,
please contact the Sterling Special Sales Department at 800-805-5489 or
specialsales@sterlingpub.com

Many talented people ___ed us cr___ ___s book (it goes to show ___ of a great network!). We'd like to thank Harvey Laney, whose tireless work and dedication were essential to this book. We're eternally grateful for the hard work and wisdom of Project Manager Amy Werner, as well as that of our colleagues at Yahoo! HotJobs, including George Toland, Douglas Lee, Lauren Meller, Yahoo! Legal, Libby Sartain, the Yahoo! Talent Acquisition team and our former colleagues Erin Hovanec, Jason Gasdick, and Christopher Jones. We'd also like to thank the staff of Barnes & Publishing, including: our devoted editor, Meredith Peters Hale; our publisher, Michael Fragnito, Production Manager Paulette Hodge; Creative Director Jeffrey Batzli; Designer Wendy Ralphs; Managing Editor Maria Spano; Pamela Wong; the agent for this series, John C. Leonhardt; and Stacey May and Amy King for the book's elegant and efficient design. Many thanks to the following for their input: Cheryl Ferguson, Andy Misovec, Melody Hudson, Judi Carey, Phil Fuhrer, and Dr. James Lea. Last but not least, we'd like to thank our families and friends for their support and inspiration.

Introduction: Heading the Pack

Buck was in open revolt. He wanted, not to escape a clubbing, but to have the leadership. It was his by right. He had earned it, and he would not be content with less.

—*Jack London,* Call of the Wild

If you're not the lead dog, so the adage goes, the view never changes. And let's face it—coveting a better view is only natural, particularly when it comes to the workplace. Depending on how long you've been in your current position (or how long you were in your last position, if you resigned or were laid off), an executive position may even feel like a birthright.

Our social order is founded on the idea of securing your place at the head of the pack. Generations of Americans have been (and still are) raised with the belief that success means achieving more than your parents did. Twenty or twenty-five years ago, high school valedictorians earned perfect 4.0 grade point averages; today they seek "hyper-perfect" 4.6s with a handful of college credits under their belts before their senior proms. It's no wonder American workplaces are so competitive, and virtually everyone wants to climb as high as he or she can up the chain of command.

Buying this book means you're ready to improve your own status, and attain a high-level position that you believe you've earned. Whether you're a currently employed up-and-comer or a recently laid-off executive hoping to get back on track, you're eyeing not just a new position, but a position of real significance. You're considering a move into the stratosphere of corporate management. You've paid your dues; now it's time to reap the rewards. But how do you get there?

Here's the good news: You're not alone in wanting to land a top-level position. If you're employed, there's a good chance your employer wants exactly the same thing for you. Top companies understand the importance of training *you* to take over one day. In fact, businesses consistently list grooming leadership from within as one of their primary challenges.

That's where you come in. After all, if corporate America wants leaders, and you want to *be* a leader, it's a win-win situation for everyone. Right?

Well, it's not quite that simple. You won't be handed a plum vice presidency and the keys to the executive washroom just because you've put your time in. If it were that easy, business hierarchies would be top-heavy with upper management and light on employees to manage. You have to *earn* your shot at the corner office, and competition is all around you—on the inside *and* on the outside. Remember, there are many executives still jobless and searching for their next positions after the economic downturn of the past few years. You may even be one of them.

Recognize, also, that while many companies like to promote from within, they are also quick to look for outside help. In fact, some companies prefer the fresh perspective a new face brings to the table, particularly in economically troubled industries. While this can be an obstacle if you're looking to advance within your company, it offers hope if you're seeking a leadership position in a new organization.

With all the challenges out there, your quest for upper management cannot be made halfheartedly or half-seriously. Much like politicians who rise from seats on county boards to positions in state governments and eventually break into the national arena, moving into the corner office requires a carefully plotted strategy that's always focused on your ultimate goal. You can't afford a "Well, I'll just give it my best shot" mentality; you have to plan each step, consider ways around every obstacle, prepare for every scenario, and hope that a little luck is on your side.

In this book, you'll discover some essential strategies that will help position you to take that next big step in your career—whether it's from middle manager to emerging executive, a parallel move between two companies, or a new position after a lengthy layoff. You'll learn:

- ☼ How to identify (and avoid) career-killing traits, people, and practices

- ☼ The art of recognizing opportunity in not-so-obvious situations

- ☼ Tools smart managers use to advance their careers

- ☼ What "branding" yourself can do for your career

- ☼ Why being patient with your current firm may be the right path to take— and if it isn't, the telltale signs that it's time to leave

- ☼ How to negotiate your executive compensation package

In the process, we'll give you tips on how to explore the hidden job market, the importance of networking and how to make it work best for you, resume and interview secrets that may surprise you, and, finally, the first actions you should take once you land the job of your dreams.

You believe in your leadership ability; now it's time to make others believe in it. You'll settle for nothing less. For that reason, this book is for you.

CHAPTER 1

Who Am I?
Why Am I Here?:
Plotting Your Course

uring the 1992 presidential election, Admiral James Stockdale—Ross Perot's unconventional choice as a running mate—uttered these words as a means of introducing himself to the American public: "Who am I? Why am I here?" Stockdale meant to come across as self-deprecating. Unfortunately, he succeeded too well; everything he said afterward—whether he was making a statement about his accomplishments or spelling out his qualifications to become vice president—was forgotten. America's enduring image of Stockdale, from that moment on, was that of a befuddled and out-of-place political pretender.

Strike "unbridled self-deprecation" from your list of desirable traits for aspiring leaders. Instead, there are a slew of other traits you *do* want to cultivate. In this chapter we'll explore the traits you'll need to make that corner office your own, evaluate your weaknesses and how to overcome them, and discuss ways to reinvent yourself as you take the next great step in your career.

THE MARK OF LEADERSHIP

What are the most important leadership qualities? The answer largely depends on whom you're asking. As far as those you will lead are concerned, polls have found that the most important qualities are things like honesty, character, and integrity. On the other hand, those you will report to—whether it's the company CEO or a board of directors—want somebody with vision, a proven performance record, and the ability to handle a crisis.

So where do the following qualities fit in?

Creativity	Forcefulness	Experience
Knowledge	Flexibility	Problem-solving ability
Initiative	Persistence	Communicative skills
Risk-taking	Innovation	Confidence
Collaboration	Adaptability	Drive
Accountability	Optimism	Motivational ability

These traits—and others—all play roles in effective leadership. Rarely will one individual embody all these qualities; even the best leaders have areas of defi-ciency. Additionally, every company values each quality differently. A business struggling to keep up with its competitors may seek innovation, while one sad-dled by recent leadership scandals may place accountability highest on its list of priorities.

Want to enhance your attractiveness as a corner-office candidate? You'll need to work on developing all of the above skills and more, focusing the greatest attention on those qualities you believe will pay the biggest dividends in your particular job search. Problem is, you're far from an objective observer when it comes to evaluating your abilities and work habits. (After all, don't all of us describe ourselves as "dedicated," "hard-working," and "persistent" during a job interview?)

Even asking your friends to critique your strengths and weaknesses won't help much. To get a true picture of your strong points and shortcomings, you need to turn to a neutral third party and Corporate America's favorite dirty little word: *assessment.*

Nobody likes assessment tests. We're confident you didn't, either, as you came through the ranks of middle management and endured everything from Myers-Briggs to Keirsey to Bar-On EQ-I. Frequently, these tests reveal a side of you that you either didn't know existed or you didn't want to face—or both.

Unfortunately, businesses love assessments. While executive candidates typically aren't asked to undergo formal testing, don't be surprised if, during the interview process, you are asked questions that appear to have no right or wrong answers. These kinds of interview questions figure in an informal assessment process designed to reveal your strengths (and expose your weaknesses) as a leader.

NO RIGHT ANSWERS

What is the correct response to the following multiple-choice question?

To ensure getting the respect of my staff, I would:
  A. *emphasize office rules*
  B. *train employees to work on their own*
  C. *eliminate ineffective employees quickly*
        —*From* Walden Personnel Testing and Consulting

All three are viable options that could earn you the respect of your subordinates, and the "proper" answer depends on the current culture at your place of work—or, more to the point, the place where you hope to work. On the surface, answer "B" would most likely earn respect rather than disdain (which could be the result of option A) or fear (which option C would likely foster). But if you've just assumed a leadership role in a floundering company and you're charged with righting the ship immediately, both A and C may be more effective "real-life" management strategies.

That ambiguity, in a nutshell, highlights why assessment tools are disliked by those who take them. The "right" answer depends on variables that may not be readily apparent. It's a far cry from the early days of your career, when the right answers were often obvious.

For example: Let's assume you started your career as a widget maker. During the initial interview process, you completed an assessment survey (or, at the very least, a job application) designed to determine the answers to two basic questions:

- ☼ Can this person make widgets?

- ☼ Can this person make *quality* widgets that will earn money for this company?

Nothing else really mattered at that point, because other people—your supervisors as well as the corporate officers—were in charge of every other aspect of your job. The expectations of the position you sought were few, they were well known, and they were easily identifiable. If for some reason you couldn't discern what was expected of you, a whole team of supervisors was ready to step in and tell you.

But things are different now. You're not interviewing for an entry-level widget-making position. You're hoping to be named the vice president of North American widget operations. Suddenly, there are a whole slew of questions your company wants answered about your leadership abilities. And every answer (as in our example above) looks feasible.

Here's the good news: At the executive level, if you *are* asked to take a formal assessment test, view it as a positive sign. The primary purpose of assessment testing is not to identify worthy candidates for advancement; in most cases, the tests are too cost-prohibitive to give to every corner-office hopeful. Instead, assessments are used to validate someone's existing belief in your capabilities. So you've already been identified as material for the corner office.

TESTING YOU CAN TAKE

Unlike the tests you took in school, you can't "cram" for most assessments or assessment-type questions. You can, however, become more familiar with them while at the same time learning more about yourself.

The following tests (or sample tests) are available online and offer an instant, if somewhat generic, appraisal of your abilities. Once you've got a grasp on your talents and tendencies, you will be better able to take advantage of your strengths—or reinvent yourself as needed, as we'll discuss in the next section.

One caveat: These are online tests; use them to get a general idea of your attributes, and don't read too much into the results. If you want a more formal assessment of your potential, your best course of action is to complete one of the more widely used diagnostic tools, such as the Myers-Briggs Type Indicator, the Keirsey Temperament Sorter, the Bar-On EQ-I, and the Thomas-Kilmann Conflict Mode Instrument. Costs of these tests range from free to hundreds, or even thousands, of dollars.

Here are some popular online assessment tests:

1. Motivational Appraisal of Personal Potential (MAPP)
   (www.assessment.com)
   In about fifteen minutes, you can complete this free, seventy-one-question test and view a bare-bones evaluation of your answers. Various packages are available, including an "executive package." The MAPP is an excellent starting point for workers hoping to determine where their strengths lie.

2. Management Development Questionnaire (MDQ)
   (http://harcourtassessment.com)
   The MDQ provides feedback on a variety of factors, including risk-taking, teamwork, flexibility, and how well you project leadership.

3. Career Advancement Test, Queendom.com
   (http://www.queendom.com/tests/career)
   There's a small fee to access this test, which evaluates your ability to assume more responsibility, responses to challenges, and drive and initiative. In addition to providing an overall score, the CAT will give you "subscores" in a variety of areas such as risk-taking, adaptability, and untapped potential.

REINVENT YOURSELF

Got a better grip on who you are? Good! You'll need it in order to mold yourself into the best candidate for any and every position you'll pursue—and in each case, you may need to emphasize certain assets and downplay others.

For example, an assessment may have revealed that "In times of conflict, I try to get along rather than rock the boat." Taken to the extreme, this could mean that you frequently give in to others, and in a crisis, you might not be willing to take the helm. However, it certainly isn't a sign that you can't lead. In fact, team-building and seeking common ground are vital leadership traits, particularly when staff tensions are running high. It's up to you to determine whether the position you covet requires a team-builder (which your answer suggests that you are) or a forceful commander.

Of course, some characteristics rarely serve you well. You can't have frequent personality conflicts with your coworkers, for instance. You can't enter panic mode whenever deadlines loom. You can't be indecisive during a crisis. These are all traits that will stifle a promising career.

Everyone—every single worker—possesses enough flaws to effectively end his or her candidacy for the corner office. How, then, do people ascend to leadership positions? The secret lies in eliminating "killer" flaws and finding the hidden advantages in other, less-damaging faults.

▶ Action Items: Eliminating "Killer" Flaws

Make a list of your top five business-related shortcomings:

1. _____

2. _____

3. _____

4. _____

5. _____

Now evaluate each shortcoming listed above, and ask yourself if it can be used to a leader's advantage. For example: Perhaps you sometimes strike coworkers as being too brusque; yet you have also earned a reputation as a "no-nonsense" manager who achieves consistent results that cast your department in a positive light. If you can't find a positive application for one of the traits you listed, it's probably a "killer flaw" and needs to be eliminated.

An important aspect of progressing in your career involves "reinventing" your work persona so that others see you in a new light. Reinvention also applies to career switchers. In the aftermath of the dot-com bust and the ensuing hike in unemployment, many executives found it necessary to consider jobs in unfamiliar industries or with corporations possessing drastically different workplace cultures. Even if you remain with your current employer, reinvention is necessary to stay on the corporate radar screen. Others must see that you have what it takes to succeed at the next level.

Workplaces are and always will be works-in-progress. They have to meet changing client demands, master evolving technologies, and accomplish more with less. If your workplace must continually evolve, it follows that you need to as well. By doing so, you'll more easily establish yourself as "someone to watch" in the eyes of your supervisors. Your willingness to reinvent yourself during times of change will help you remain relevant.

But how do you do it? Here are three ways to promote the "reinvention" of your work image:

Education

Regardless of your profession, it's tough to imagine a long career if you aren't constantly learning new things. The idea that "We've always done it this way" is not only foolhardy, it's heretical. It's a cliché that shouldn't exist in any business environment. It *hasn't* always been done that way, and it *won't* be done that way in the future. For example, who would have predicted that music lovers would one day be able to hold an entire CD collection in a pants pocket? By taking advantage of evolving technologies, Steve Jobs and Apple have been able to revolutionize the way that customers purchase and experience music. And even Steve Jobs hasn't stopped learning from and improving on his accomplishments, following up the phenomenally successful iPod with the iPod mini, the iPod shuffle, and the iPod nano.

Stay abreast of developing practices in your line of work. Seek them out. Learn from past mistakes; learn from your competitors; and learn from small, everyday experiences. Learn because education is the driving force behind business evolution. Remember, the first affordable VCR was a Sony Betamax; at the start of the personal computing revolution, programmers used a language called FORTRAN. What if learning had stopped in either of those industries?

Responsibility

Your immediate supervisors are constantly directed to do more with less, because by doing so they make the business more profitable. It can be a very difficult order to fill at times. By asking for more responsibilities—or tackling new, previously unassigned tasks as they come in—you'll earn a reputation as a team member committed to putting the organization first.

Does this also make your boss look good? Sure it does, and there's a chance your efforts may actually help launch her into upper management. That's not such a bad thing for you, however. She will want to keep you extremely close on the way up.

take a memo

Learn from Your Mistakes

Be willing to make mistakes, perhaps in colossal fashion. Venturing into new territory sometimes calls for a mistakes-be-damned attitude, which is acceptable as long as you learn from your errors and rectify them as quickly as possible. In 1985, the Coca-Cola Company introduced New Coke in an effort to reverse a continuing free-fall in sales, as soft-drink rival Pepsi gained market share at Coke's expense. Despite careful market research, it was a disastrous, ill-conceived idea that tanked immediately. Quick response by Coca-Cola, however, led to the return of the original formula (this time called "Coke Classic") less than three months later. In an ironic footnote, soon after its reintroduction, Coke Classic gained the top-selling soft-drink slot that New Coke had been created to win.

Profitability

Businesses love to talk about things like community involvement and other altruistic goals. At the end of the day, however, the business is about the bottom line. Profits are the fuel that powers the engine to pursue philanthropic ventures, and (more importantly) they allow your company to increase its market share.

If you gain a reputation as someone who provides more fuel to the engine in your current position, you won't have to clamor too loudly for an opportunity to move ahead—your company will trip over itself to find one for you. It's difficult to impact your firm's revenues in a staff position, so seek line positions—those that have budgetary and fiscal responsibilities. An overwhelming number of future leaders are culled from line jobs because they've already demonstrated the ability to make money.

Keep corporate prosperity in mind as you plot your career path, because filling your employer's coffers has always been a fast-track route to senior management.

DAMAGE CONTROL

As Sinatra once sang, "Regrets, I've had a few. . . ." Doubtless you have a few regrets of your own as well, whether you're a longtime employee with your current company or you're planning a fresh start with another organization.

Some catastrophic career moves (such as being caught engaging in illegal or unethical behavior) can't be undone. With these types of missteps in your past, even Enron may not trust you with a high-level position. Remember that integrity and honesty are at the top of the leadership wish list. Short of criminal behavior, however, the damage done by most indiscretions can be overcome. For an honest evaluation of the obstacles ahead, ask yourself the following questions:

- ☼ Do you have a reputation for treating your subordinates badly?
- ☼ Do peers in other departments accuse you of being an empire builder (or a talent raider)?
- ☼ Do you have a difficult time bringing a project in under budget, or on time?
- ☼ Have you been heard badmouthing top executives?
- ☼ Do you have a reputation as being somewhat undependable?
- ☼ Are you simply too "nice" to move into an executive position?

Discover the "skeletons" in your closet in advance. Be thorough; it won't do you much good to wear blinders now if these allegations are going to come up during a job interview. Before proceeding with your executive job search, determine a satisfactory response for each one. In many cases, you're dealing more with perception than reality, but perception is reality until you alter it. For example, you can change the perception that you're too confrontational for a leadership position with one or two interviews where you exhibit grace and diplomacy.

Overstaying Your Welcome

In an ideal world, your first employer is your employer for life. You move continually and rapidly up the corporate ladder. Those above you value each and every piece of input you provide. Those below you are grateful to be working with you. Your career path is not only clearly outlined from the first day you start work, it is unwavering.

In reality, if any of those situations ever existed in the first place, it's extremely unlikely they will continue over the course of your ascendancy to upper management. At some point, you will face the very real prospect that to get ahead, you have to get out.

Leaving your employer may be a wise career move; then again, staying put (even if you are passed over for a promotion) may be the better choice. If you are currently employed, take a look at your present situation and ask yourself these questions:

☼ Is there a glut of leadership candidates in this company whose qualifications are roughly equal to mine?

☼ Can I successfully meet the expectations this company has for its leaders?

☼ What is the timeframe for "leadership turnover" here?

☼ How big of a role will office politics play in promotions—and if it's truly a political process, how will I fare?

☼ Will my current boss support me in my efforts to move up the corporate ladder?

☼ Can I be happy here if I am passed over for a management position?

☼ If I am passed over now, when will the next position become available?

Once you've analyzed your employer, you can better analyze your career. In some cases, you may decide that sitting tight is your best option. On the other hand, many professionals have discovered that they have to move on to move ahead, so don't despair if that's the conclusion you reach.

hot facts

Executive Search by the Numbers

Take a purely numerical look at executive job-hunting:

57 Percentage of executives who considered themselves "in transition" in 2005—a decrease from 2003's finding of 74 percent. However . . .

28 This percentage considered themselves "employed and actively in a job search"—twice as many as in 2003.

2.8 Average number of years after which executives surveyed said they change jobs. (They change companies every 3.6 years.)

4.5 Number of years, on average, executives expected to remain in their next position. (They expected to spend 5.4 years at their next company.)

(Source: ExecuNet's 2005 Executive Job Market Intelligence Report.)

Staying Put

When Karla accepted a promotion in the sales department of a pharmaceutical firm, she was excited by the opportunity it represented. At the same time, she realized that many of the senior sales representatives there had been in their positions for several years, while she hoped to use her new position as a springboard to a higher office.

Worried that she would be "back-burnered" in her new job, she sought the advice of a coworker who had worked in the same department and had recently landed an upper-management position. His advice was succinct: Give the new job two years. If, after two years, Karla was still in her current position, she should assume that she would always be in it and start looking elsewhere for advancement. On the other hand, if her responsibilities and title evolved during that two-year period, it would be a sign that her patience and work ethic would eventually be rewarded.

Armed with her colleague's advice, Karla concentrated on the job at hand. With about four months remaining on her two-year, self-imposed limit, her consistantly strong performance won her a management position in a newly created department.

Of course, every worker's circumstances are unique. What worked for Karla may not work for you. Unlike Karla, your analysis of your current situation may point you toward the exit.

Moving Out

Grant, a graphic artist, was every manager's dream: punctual, talented, dedicated, and a consummate team player. He was aware of his reputation as a reliable employee and believed it was enough to ensure his eventual rise into upper management.

After four years, despite positive annual performance evaluations and corresponding pay increases, Grant found himself wondering why he had yet to receive a promotion. Unbeknownst to him, a specific—and insurmountable—obstacle stood between him and a leadership position. His immediate supervisor's boss was adamant that Grant had peaked as an employee, going as far as to say, "If Grant wants to sit here and work our graphics desk until the day he dies, I'll let him."

Only after speaking with his manager did Grant learn of the comment; obviously, in order to advance he would have to change companies. He did so shortly afterward.

From the Desk of

Margaret Kelly
CEO, RE/MAX International

I began at RE/MAX International in 1987 as a financial analyst— not even a managerial position. I had been in management at a previous company, but chose to go to RE/MAX because I saw enormous potential, not only for me personally, but for the organization as a whole.

I recognized right away that RE/MAX was a unique organization, one in which individuals had every chance to rise as high as their ability and ambition would take them. I believed there would be no constraints, no glass ceiling. I believed loyalty would be rewarded.

That's exactly the way it has been. Since RE/MAX was founded in 1973, we've had six presidents and four CEOs, and every one has been home-grown.

Almost all of our senior managers have come from within. We think it works better that way, both for us and for our franchisees. They like the continuity and the sense of family it entails.

We're confident that we already have our next generation of leaders on board.

What do we look for when we consider potential managers?

We look for people who don't believe their own press, so to speak. They have the attitude that they're not too good to do anything. Since there's no job they wouldn't do themselves, there's nothing they couldn't ask somebody else to do.

They don't demand respect, they earn it.

They have the attitude that they don't work *for* anybody, and nobody works *for* them—we all work together.

We're not afraid to ask our employees to stretch their abilities and respond to a challenge. Some do and some don't; but when you find somebody who does step up, you've really got something.

RE/MAX is one of the largest real estate networks in the world.

Can you move up or should you move out? It's a question only you can answer. If you decide to move on, always remember the most important proverb . . .

It's a Small World

What? Did you think we were going to tell you not to burn your bridges? Actually, the messages of both sayings are nearly identical. Both caution against treating people poorly now, because there's a good chance your paths will cross again. But historically, "burning your bridges" didn't mean eliminating your return path; it meant covering your tracks so your enemy couldn't follow you.

Conversely, "It's a small world" simply means you will cross paths again. Trust us—you will. At the very least, you might. Either way, a good departure, with no ill will on either side, is vital.

ASSESSMENT IS ONLY THE FIRST CHALLENGE

Whew! You haven't even begun your job search, and already you're inundated with a roster of tasks to complete in your quest for a high-level position. In the next chapter, we'll give you an overview of what to expect as you proceed in your search, and recommendations on how to handle each challenge you come across. Recognize that it's hard work being an executive, and it takes hard work to land a job as one. The rewards, however, are plentiful for those who succeed.

Recommended Books

Career Assessments and Their Meanings by Ellyn Sanna (Mason Crest Publishers, 2002, ISBN 1590843096, $22.95).

Discover What You're Best At: A Complete Career System That Lets You Test Yourself to Discover Your Own True Career Abilities by Linda Gale (Simon & Schuster, 1998, ISBN 0684839563, $14.00).

Handbook of U.S. Labor Statistics 2005 by Eva A. Jacobs and Mary Meghan Ryan, eds. (Almanac Publishing, Inc., 2005, ISBN 1886222207, $147.00).

Nobodies to Somebodies: How 100 Great Careers Got Their Start by Peter Han (Portfolio, 2005, ISBN 1591840864, $22.95).

The Play of Your Life: Your Program for Finding the Career of Your Dreams—And a Step-by-step Guide to Making It a Reality by Colleen A. Sabatino (Rodale Press, Inc., 2004, ISBN 1579549640, $16.95).

Recommended Web Sites

Queendom.com—Career Assessment Test:
http://www.queendom.com/tests/career/career_adv_access.html

Management Development Questionnaire:
http://harcourtassessment.com

Motivational Appraisal of Personal Potential:
http://www.assessment.com

U.S. Department of Labor Programs and Surveys:
http://stats.bls.gov/bls/proghome.htm

Bureau of Labor Statistics: Occupational Outlook Handbook for Top Executives:
http://stats.bls.gov/oco/ocos012.htm

2

Experience, Challenges, and Experiencing Challenges

"I usually wake up screaming at six-thirty, and I'm in my office by nine."

A s you've learned from past experience, finding a job is never easy. You wouldn't be reading this book right now if the task were relatively straightforward and trouble-free.

But as difficult as finding a job may be, landing one is even tougher. There are many steps between wanting a job and winning a job, and each has the potential to turn into a misstep. At the very least, each phase of your quest for the corner office contains hurdles you may not have anticipated or encountered in previous job hunts.

This chapter serves as a brief introduction to the process of job searching at this level. You'll see frequent cross-references to sections found elsewhere, allowing you to quickly find additional information of particular interest to you—because, no matter how great your past accomplishments are or how much experience you've gained, you will run into obstacles on the way to the top:

  ☼ Available jobs are not always advertised.

  ☼ Your search may have to be done in a clandestine fashion.

  ☼ The job search itself will take much longer than you expect.

  ☼ You may feel underqualified for the openings you find.

  ☼ Your candidacy will be scrutinized vigilantly.

  ☼ The interview process is multilayered and repetitious.

  ☼ Delays in decision making are common.

  ☼ The hiring process may involve steps you've never encountered before.

By recognizing the challenges of your job search in advance and preparing beforehand, you'll be better able to weather the process. We can't say you'll enjoy it—but you'll survive it, and in the end that's what matters most.

MINING FOR GOLD

Some of the available jobs at the executive level are not publicized because there's no need for them to be publicized. When corporations look outside their own walls for new leaders, positions may be filled through the use of an executive recruiter (which we will discuss at length in chapter 3); vacancies that are filled through internal promotion, of course, need not be advertised either.

How, then, do you sniff out the openings? The following are some of the fastest paths to the corner office.

From the Desk of

Elizabeth Kanna
Dream Maker and Cofounder, *Dream In You*

My life changed in an instant eight years ago. While reading one night, I encountered a familiar quote—and its significance ignited a long-forgotten passion. I grabbed a pen and paper, and I captured the vision of what I wanted my life to be. This vision set in motion a personal and professional transformation.

I'm often asked, *"How did you do it? How did you create your dream?"* That night I vowed to let passion guide, inspire, and shield that vision against the dream killers we all have: well-meaning friends, coworkers, life situations, and our own fears. No more would dream killers stop me from creating work that I was passionate about that also utilized my talents and gifts.

If you decide to change employers, go for that significant promotion with the corner office, or change industries altogether—go for it with passion. Your passion will set you apart from the pack, and inspire those around you. JetBlue CEO David Neeleman's passion continually inspires his employees to reinvent the airline industry. His notable success depends on having enough passion to inspire his team to achieve great things. People catch on to the vision of dedicated leaders who transform their industry—or the world.

Do you really want that corner office or VP position? Discover—or rediscover—your true passion. Try these exercises: Close your eyes, and in your mind and heart live your idea of a perfect day in which you're doing work you love. See every detail of that day. Next, think about inheriting $10 million. After several months (or several years) of traveling, sitting on the beach, and playing, what would you do next? Hidden somewhere within these reflections is the key to your passion.

And if, perchance, you discover that you're not passionate about your current job, go for the dream job—with or without the corner office.

The quote? "Go confidently in the direction of your dreams. Live the life you have imagined."—Henry David Thoreau

Dream In You is a consulting firm that helps individuals transform their professional lives.

Networking

Many executives find their jobs through networking. The Old Boy Network is alive and well, although these days it contains both sexes and countless niches. With a little bit of searching, you can find highly organized networks tailored to individuals by age, industry, geography, ethnicity, salary range, and other factors. Chapter 5 explores networking opportunities more fully.

Executive Recruiters   .

Because corporations like to use executive search firms, you need to use them as well. Otherwise, your potential candidacy for a plum assignment may never bloom into anything substantial (such as an interview). Recruiters continually seek out would-be executives; after all, their livelihood depends on maintaining a well-stocked pool of contenders. If recruiters reach out to you, you'd be wise to consider using their services. If you haven't been approached, perhaps you're flying under their radar. In chapter 3, we provide an overview of the recruiting industry and how it can help you land the position you want. We'll also talk about publicizing your availability and qualifications to help you attract the attention of search firms.

Internet

What did we do before this became such a dominant presence in our lives? In addition to advertising hundreds of thousands of available jobs, sites like Yahoo! HotJobs are gold mines of information on everything from interviewing to negotiating benefits and bonuses. For industry information, career advice, and job openings, the Internet should be a frequent destination as you search for a new leadership position. Recruiters are also known to rely heavily on the Web to find executive-level candidates. Don't confine your online work to perusing job databases and researching potential employers—create your own Web page or blog (but be sure it only contains information you want your employer or future employer to see). This kind of Internet showcase not only provides a convenient portal for your resume, but also gives you a forum to instantly highlight your most recent accomplishments. An extra benefit: It points up your ability to market yourself effectively. We'll talk more about applying for jobs over the Internet in chapter 6.

Print Advertising

Executive-level positions *are* advertised in more targeted publications. Check out industry-specific periodicals and newsletters, as well as local and national business journals that cater to executive readers. Even your company newsletter could tip you off to openings that may be imminent because of newly created divisions or product lines.

⚡THINK Outside the Box 💡

Corporate and Employee Blogs

At first glance, blogs and corporate America would seem to be odd dance partners. Blogs, after all, are the most recent incarnation of a truly free and unrestricted press, while most major corporations have regulations limiting what their employees can say publicly or to media organizations. But there are a surprising number of corporate blog sites, and the trend is on the rise. If you're considering a move to a specific company, a tour of the postings on its blog site could give you a revealing glimpse into its workplace culture. (To find a directory of corporate blog sites, see the "Recommended Web Sites" section at the end of this chapter.)

In addition to corporate blogs, consider investigating *employee* blogs. Even if you can't find a blog maintained by someone in upper management, any employee's blog can offer hints as to the *real* atmosphere within a company, or how other people working there perceive the organization. While the information is unfiltered, it may offer valuable insight.

Other Means

Be proactive in your search. It's possible that a company's leaders may not even know they need a position filled—until you tell them what they're missing. Research businesses that interest you and determine whether they could do things more efficiently in an area that matches your special skill set. Anticipate change within a corporation; if you read in the *Wall Street Journal* that Tom's T-Shirts, Inc. hopes to expand its product line into the uniform industry next year, send in your resume along with a cover letter spelling out how you can help ensure a successful transition for the company into that area.

TIME MARCHES ON (AND ON, AND ON, AND ON . . .)

According to Challenger, Gray & Christmas, an outplacement and consulting company, the average duration of an executive-level job search is almost four months. Patience is not only a virtue; it's a requirement when you're trying to climb the next rung of the corporate ladder. In general, the loftier a position is, the more time it will take to fill it. Much of this time is consumed by behind-the-scenes machinations; for example, a company may know six months out that its vice president of marketing is retiring at year's end, although Joe Stockholder and even staffers within the firm are unaware of this. Because you're a candidate, you'll be interviewed (and reinterviewed—more on that later) well in advance of the job's opening date. Prepare yourself for a lengthy process.

Other factors can add to the overall time needed before you receive the keys to the corner office. Many upper-level positions require a vote by a search committee or a board of directors, and such votes can be delayed by the availability of committee members, market circumstances, or other factors.

take a memo

Big Brother Is Watching

If becoming a corporate executive means you'll have to leave your current employer, be very careful when conducting your search. Do not use your current business e-mail account as a means of communication. According to the American Management Association, almost 75 percent of major U.S. companies say they review staff e-mail, Web usage, and telephone use on a regular basis as a security measure, and courts have consistently ruled that businesses have the right to snoop into their employees' e-mail accounts. This "snooping" isn't limited to your e-mail account; avoid using your office computer and phone for job searching as well, because improper usage might endanger your current position.

TALK TO ME (AND ME, AND ME, AND ME . . .)

Remember that first job interview years ago? You worked yourself into a frenzy preparing for it, only to discover it was only fifteen minutes of relatively straightforward questioning. It was quick and to the point because studies suggest that most interviewers make a decision on a candidate's desirability within the first five minutes.

Unlike those early career days, now it is likely that you'll meet people from many different departments (such as sales, marketing, finance, and others). Think of upper-management interviewing as surviving the gauntlet; once you've passed muster with your initial interviewer, you'll be passed on to others. Be consistent in your answers. Each interviewer will likely share her thoughts about her talk with you before the employer reaches a final decision on whether to hire you. Chapter 8 offers an in-depth look at the intricacies of interviewing at this level.

UNDER THE MICROSCOPE

In addition to a more involved interview process, you can expect all areas of your life to come under careful scrutiny. Companies are increasingly moving beyond basic reference checks and into areas heretofore reserved for political candidates. Conducting full-scale background checks is becoming standard operating procedure in the vetting process. These inquiries may probe your legal history and your credit record, require personality and intelligence testing, delve into your club and association memberships, and more.

Are there skeletons in your closet? For example, have you had to overcome a past addiction to gambling or alcohol? Have you been named in any work-related criminal or civil lawsuits? You may think some facets of your private life are off-limits. Your future employer probably doesn't share that point of view.

Potential employers may ask for your consent to conduct an investigation. Of course, they may not consider your application if you don't consent, so you're really not in a position to say no. What you can do, however, is make sure everything is in order or can be explained satisfactorily.

Some past problems may derail your job search and may take time to overcome. The case of Jack, a public relations specialist, offers insight into one such situation. Jack's talent was unquestionable, and he moved quickly up the ladder at a nationally recognized PR firm. But as Jack approached the senior-management level, excessive drinking began taking its toll. While being considered for an open vice presidency slot, Jack drank too heavily one night and landed in jail.

The incident obviously ended any hopes he had of winning the position. But it did serve as a long-needed wake-up call. With his employer's support, Jack took a leave of absence to enter rehab. When he returned to work, he did so (by agreement) in a subordinate role, where he had experienced so much of his early success. Over time, his responsibilities increased until he reached his previous level of employment. Instead of stumbling, however, Jack now had the strength to handle the pressures and responsibilities he faced without resorting to alcohol.

Jack may never leave his current employer because of a strong sense of gratitude he feels for the support he received when he was in trouble. He also knows that if he *does* choose to pursue work with another firm, he'll likely have to deal with questions about his past drinking problems. However, he is hopeful that his most recent performance will outweigh past misdeeds—the "What have you done for me lately?" syndrome, as he likes to call it.

take a **memo**

The Fair Credit Reporting Act

The federal Fair Credit Reporting Act (FCRA) requires employers to obtain written consent from applicants or employees before researching an employee or prospective employee's credit report or conducting a background check for "employment purposes." This covers hiring decisions as well as the process of evaluating employees for promotion or reassignment.

Scrutinize Your References

Only an extreme novice would provide a prospective employer with an unenthusiastic reference, right? But your references could be asked a wide range of questions, including many you might not anticipate. A favorite tack for recruiters and employers is to end their discussions with your references by seeking three *additional* references.

That's exactly what happened when Beth applied for a position as an industry analyst with a North Carolina company. Her references checked out fine, but when a secondary reference was contacted, he responded to the recruiter's mention of Beth's name by saying, "What? I can't believe you'd even think of hiring her."

Interview your references in advance. What are they willing to say about you? Which questions would they prefer not to answer? Find out which names they would provide as secondary references, and then go through the same process with those contacts.

Know Thyself

Before you allow others to pry into your past, do it yourself. For a couple of hundred dollars, you can use the same investigating firms many companies use to verify your credit rating, employment history, criminal record, and other aspects of your life. The peace of mind you'll receive through this exercise is invaluable, and you may even discover errors that can be corrected before you undergo a corporate background check. Some "innocent" errors on these types of reports include inverted Social Security numbers or information about individuals with a similar name as yours. A list of investigative resources is included at the end of this chapter.

hot facts

Credit Report Errors

Check your credit report annually. A 2004 study by the national arm of the Public Interest Research Group found that almost 80 percent of U.S. credit reports contained some type of error, ranging from misspelled names to duplicate loan listings to information belonging to another person. Almost 25 percent contained errors serious enough to warrant the denial of a loan—or a job offer.

Be Forthright

Everyone makes mistakes, and you are entitled to yours. Millions of American workers deal with everything from alcohol and drug addiction to other problems that can derail their careers.

You could try to hide your past demons if you have them, but there's a very good chance they'll be discovered anyway—and that would be career suicide. Plus, you never know how vigilant investigators for a rival firm may be—it would be disastrous to land a job, only to have a major mistake from your past revealed by your new company's competition. Not only would you do irreparable damage to your own career, but you could possibly drag your company (and its reputation) down with you.

A better approach is to be open about your past without providing half-hearted excuses or "explanations" about how you really weren't to blame. By being candid, you eliminate any fears you may have about certain incidents being discovered, and you also cast yourself as someone with honesty and integrity—two essential components of leadership. You can enhance this perception by taking proactive steps to ensure that past mistakes won't be repeated. For example, it's admirable to overcome a substantial drug addiction. It's even better if you can follow that up by citing your volunteer efforts to help other drug users come clean.

One caveat: If your past contains an event that you believe most employers would have difficulty ignoring and you're already employed, you may want to reevaluate your job search in the first place. You may be better off quietly appreciating the job you have, rather than risking everything by trying to rise even higher. Flying under the radar only works when you don't make an effort to soar.

take a memo

Overcoming a Layoff or Termination

Bad things sometimes happen to good people. The good news: In today's economy, layoffs are fairly easy to explain. Workers sidelined by a layoff are typically seen as victims of circumstances beyond their control. The bad news: Terminations are a completely different story. On the positive side, the threat of a possible lawsuit may keep many employers from discussing why you are no longer employed—they'll usually provide employment dates during a reference check, but little else. On the negative side, you still have to explain a gap in your work history.

As we'll discuss in chapter 6, employment gaps are difficult to explain within the resume itself, but can be handled in a well-worded cover letter; doing so will help a recruiter or hiring manager ignore nagging doubts created by the missing dates. Use the interview to more fully explain the circumstances surrounding your departure and summarize what you've learned from the experience.

WHY YOU?

Most leaders (particularly reluctant leaders) have faced the "Why me?" question. It's natural to feel overmatched by a new endeavor, particularly one that is substantially more challenging than those you've tackled in the past.

When doubts arise, remember that you've worked out the answers to this question long before now. The "Why me" answers are based on desires within yourself:

☼ You want to rise within your organization's hierarchy.

☼ You are confident that a better situation is out there for you.

☼ You have supported your "gut feeling" that the timing is right by research-ing the necessary information (as evidenced by reading this book).

☼ Your decision, therefore, is based on reason, logic, and careful planning, which should ensure that your transition into upper management will be as worry-free as possible.

take a memo

Michael Jordan on Failure

During the 1997 NBA Finals between the Chicago Bulls and the Utah Jazz, a Nike ad campaign featured the following words of wisdom from basket-ball legend Michael Jordan: "I have missed more than nine thousand shots in my career. I have lost almost three hundred games. On twenty-six occa-sions I have been entrusted to take the game-winning shot and missed. And I have failed over and over and over again in my life. And that is why I succeed."

It's normal to have doubts about your ability to succeed; fear of failure is a healthy motivator. However, *keep these insecurities to yourself*. Doing so will make you appear assured and confident, traits that can help assuage any doubts in an interviewer's mind about hiring you. You don't have to meet every "requirement" listed on a job prospectus. Those represent a wish list composite of the ideal candidate, and few (if any) individuals can satisfy each item on that list.

For that reason, it is not unheard of for an underqualified candidate to win a plum assignment or promotion. (Note that we said "underqualified," not "unqualified." There's a huge difference between the two.) With the exception of entrepreneurs who launch their own companies, *every CEO in the world has been underqualified for her position at some point*, because she had never been CEO before. The same holds true for chief financial officers, vice presidents of marketing, national directors of sales, and anyone else who finds his way to the corner office for the first time.

Remember, you bring unique abilities and experiences to the table. Trust your instincts; you're ready for new responsibilities—and to face the challenges ahead.

▶**Action Item:** Make Your Case

What's the best way to address the subject of underqualification? Consider the following responses if the topic of being underqualified comes up during the interview process:

Showcase similar circumstances in the past	"I can understand your misgivings about my ability to succeed in this position. Five years ago, I was named manager of Project X by my current employer even though I was the youngest member of the management team. Here's what I did to succeed..."
Establish your willingness to learn	"As my employment history shows, continuing my education plays a major part in my work philosophy. It is a means to take on new challenges, and I expect to do the same in this position."
Express fervent enthusiasm for the position	"I am very excited about the opportunity to help your company establish itself as the market leader, and I look forward to instilling this passion in my colleagues."
Play up your soft skills	"This position appears to require a leader with team-building and interpersonal skills. In my current role, I have used those same abilities to increase sales 32 percent in the past year."
Highlight your strengths to offset minor weaknesses	"While it's true that I have never led a marketing group this large, I have considerable experience in budgeting and promotional development."

WOMEN AND MINORITIES

As a female, a member of a minority group, or both, you may face very real issues while working your way to the executive level. The bad news: Many of the barriers you might encounter are inherently unfair. The good news: Few, if any, are insurmountable. It will require diligence and commitment on your part, but take heart in the fact that others have trod the path you are approaching. Seek their advice, be aware of the perceptions you need to overcome, and stay the course. At the end of the chapter, you'll find recommended books and Web sites that address the obstacles women and minorities face in climbing the corporate ladder in the United States.

Success is color-blind; ultimately, it is dollar-driven in virtually all companies. Be cognizant of the challenges you may face, but don't obsess about sex and race. Trust us: If you produce positive results, these factors should be the last thing on an employer's mind.

hot facts ··

Minority Standings

Consider the following percentages of executive management positions (defined as jobs with any of forty-eight titles such as CEO, CFO, president, and vice president) filled by women and minorities, according to a Peopleclick Research Institute study of U.S. Census data:

> Women, 1990: 31.9%
> Women, 2000: 18.8%
> African-Americans, 1990: 13%
> African-Americans, 2000: 16.7%

Other surveys reveal similarly stark results: According to a 2005 report by Catalyst, a nonprofit research and advisory organization working to advance women in business, women and minorities hold roughly 29% of Fortune 100 board seats, with white men holding 71% of the seats. A 2003 study by the Hispanic Association on Corporate Responsibility found that Hispanics, meanwhile, hold only 1.1% of executive offices within the Fortune 1000—despite being the nation's largest minority group.

CHALLENGES MET

If you stay aware of the challenges you'll face as your job search proceeds, you should be able to survive the ordeal in good shape. It will take a long time. It will expose areas of your life (both professional and personal) that you'd rather forget but can't afford to ignore. It will foster feelings of inadequacy in your abilities (particularly as the process becomes more drawn out and arduous). In the end, however, successfully negotiating all these hurdles could leave you positioned exactly where you want to be—atop the short list of candidates for the leadership position you've coveted for a long time. Once you receive the key to your new office, you'll find that all of the above unpleasantness will have been worth it.

Recommended Books

Breaking Through: The Making of Minority Executives in Corporate America by David A. Thomas and John J. Gabarro (Harvard Business School Press, 1999, ISBN 0875848664, $29.95).

Cracking the Corporate Code: The Revealing Success Stories of 32 African-American Executives by Price M. Cobbs & Judith Turnock (AMACOM, 2003, ISBN 0814407714, $24.95).

Executive Job Search Handbook: All You Need to Make Your Move—From Marketing Yourself With a Master Resume to Networking, Targeting Companies, and Negotiating the Job Offer by Robert F. Wilson (Thomson Delmar Publishing, 2003, ISBN 1564146626, $16.99).

Fired Up!: How the Best of the Best Survived and Thrived After Getting the Boot by Harvey Mackay (Random House, 2005, ISBN 0345471873, $14.95).

Landing on the Right Side of Your Ass: A Survival Guide for the Recently Unemployed by Michael B. Laskoff (Three Rivers Press, 2004, ISBN 1400051142, $14.00).

Minority Executives' Handbook by Randolph W. Cameron (HarperCollins, 1993, ISBN 156743021X, $14.95)

Nice Girls Don't Get the Corner Office: 101 Unconscious Mistakes Women Make That Sabotage Their Careers by Lois P. Frankel (Warner Business Books, 2004, ISBN 0446531324, $19.95).

Over-40 Job Search Guide: 10 Strategies for Making Your Age an Advantage in Your Career by Gail Geary (Jist Works, 2004, ISBN 1593570902, $14.95).

Play Like a Man, Win Like a Woman: What Men Know About Success That Women Need to Learn by Gail Evans (Broadway, 2001, ISBN 076790463X $14.95).

The Secrets of Executive Search: Professional Strategies for Managing Your Personal Job Search by Robert M. Melancon (John Wiley & Sons, 2002, ISBN 0471244155, $16.95).

Secrets of Six-Figure Women: Surprising Strategies to Up Your Earnings and Change Your Life by Barbara Stanny (HarperCollins, 2002, ISBN 0060185481, $23.95).

Weddle's Guide to Employment Sites on the Internet 2005–2006 by Peter Weddle (WEDDLE's, 2005, ISBN 1928734278, $27.95).

Recommended Web Sites

Yahoo! Small Business—Domain name registration:
http://smallbusiness.yahoo.com/domains

The State PIRG Consumer Protection Inside Pages—How to contact credit agencies:
http://www.pirg.org/consumer/credit

AnnualCreditReport.com—Request free credit report:
http://www.annualcreditreport.com

National Data Research—Public record information and background searches:
http://www.search-ndr.com

CEO Update—Information on senior-level nonprofit jobs:
http://www.ceoupdate.com

Researching companies online:
http://www.learnwebskills.com
http://finance.yahoo.com

Corporate blog listings:
http://www.thenewpr.com

DiversitySearch.com—Helping to promote diversity in the workplace:
http://www.diversitysearch.com

Catalyst—Research on all aspects of women's career advancement:
http://www.catalystwomen.org

CareerWomen.com:
http://www.careerwomen.com

Yahoo! 360—Personal blog site:
http://360.yahoo.com

CHAPTER

3

Executive Recruiters: Becoming Suitable and Recruitable

"I've got an opening for a project manager in a corporation that will chew you up and spit you back out on the street in record time. Interested?"

At the end of chapter 1, we touched briefly on the possibility that you may have to look outside your current company to advance your career. We also offered some thoughts on how to determine whether it's time for you to leave. If you've decided to remain with your present employer because your prospects there are rosy, you may be tempted to skip this chapter.

Before you flip ahead to chapter 4, though, be aware that companies are increasingly looking outside their own ranks for leadership. Several factors are driving this trend, but overall what a company's decision makers are seeking from someone who's never worked there are the following: fresh vision, independent-minded leadership, strong financial skills, and the opportunity to enter a new era with a clean slate. In addition, many firms view the chance to lure a high-visibility industry leader as a way to attract more people to the company at the higher end of the talent scale—with the added benefit of simultaneously impressing shareholders and potential investors. So don't skip ahead without answering this question:

Is your company looking outside?

If it is, or even if you think it may be, a change of scenery may be necessary. This chapter is written just for you. It's all about the person (or people) best able to connect you to the corner office. It's time to meet the executive recruiter.

Your New Best Friend

Unless you married your grade-school sweetheart, someone probably introduced you to your spouse before you walked down the aisle. This, essentially, mirrors the role an executive recruiter plays in managing your career. It's a simplified analogy, to be sure, but it offers a quick glimpse into what recruiting entails. And there are a number of key parallels:

- A recruiter, much like a well-intentioned friend, recognizes the value that can come from Party A getting to know Party B.
- Each party is made aware of the existence of the other. If both parties express an interest, the recruiter (like a matchmaking friend) facilitates the introduction and (optimally) works with each side in an effort to determine whether the two of you will be compatible.

While this may be a rather rudimentary analogy, it's worth remembering—if only because some job-hunters instinctively shy away from the use of recruiters, insisting that they can handle a job search on their own. As a result, they forfeit what could be the best job-search tool at their disposal.

Sure, you can find a spouse all by yourself. Maybe even the perfect spouse. Then again, as a rule there's no deadline when you're searching for a mate, and the pursuit itself is usually enjoyable. Job searches, on the other hand, are frequently time-sensitive and rarely fun-filled. Given all that, what's not to like about going the route of an executive recruiter? Linking jobs to candidates is what these people do all day, every day. Unless you're a chronic job-hopper, finding work probably isn't your strong suit.

How Recruiting Works

Now that you understand a recruiter's basic role, it's time for more details about how recruiters operate.

A recruiter working on a contingency basis is paid only if he helps a company fill a vacancy. One working on retainer usually has an exclusive relationship with his client company and is paid (at least partially) regardless of whether he actually places a candidate in the position. And then there are in-house corporate recruiters, charged with identifying up-and-coming leaders within and outside a company. In-house recruiters can fill positions at any and all levels, depending on the company. Because they are employees, they are paid directly by their company; however, they still have to keep within their recruiting budgets.

Why does that matter to you? It doesn't, at least in terms of the professionalism you should expect and the results you're seeking. A good recruiter will focus on making the best fit possible, and she will streamline and accelerate the hiring process for her client. Therefore, her goal is to recommend people with the "right" resumes—to provide her client with quality rather than quantity. The end result for you should be the same: You should ultimately find yourself accepting the perfect job.

Why Recruiting Works

Recruiting—at least at the executive level—is a fairly new development in the history of American employment. Forty or fifty years ago, many workers expected to spend most of their careers with one or two employers; companies groomed leadership from within their own ranks. Even as recently as thirty years ago, company loyalty remained high. Everyone may not have loved where they worked, but fewer options and a nationwide economic malaise combined to keep most employees in place.

THINK Outside the Box

Using More Than One Recruiter

It may seem a bit counterintuitive to have more than one executive recruiter engaged in your job search; however, if you keep in mind how the recruitment industry works, you'll understand why enlisting the services of an additional recruiter can be beneficial.

The majority of recruiters you meet work with a clearly defined list of corporate clients. It's a safe bet that each recruiter's client list, while not mutually exclusive, is limited enough to safeguard against the unlikely event that two of them will submit your resume for the same position. So you're actually limiting your prospects by focusing all your hopes on only one recruiter; she may be able to place you with several firms within your region, even though two dozen potential employers may be out there.

We don't recommend working with more than two recruiters. And keep in mind that you need to make each recruiter aware of the other. Don't be bashful about having both recruiters actively trying to place you. Your only concern is finding the right job as quickly as possible. In cases where conflicts arise between the recruiters, it is in your best interest to make sure that matters are being handled diplomatically. Be sure to take an interest in how the conflict is resolved.

Top-level executive search firms understand that they will compete for the privilege of placing you, particularly in competitive industries or geographic regions. Any recruiters who try to dissuade you from using others should be abandoned, because their best interests obviously overshadow yours.

Fast-forward to the 1990s. A booming economy, fueled by the high-tech explosion, helped destigmatize the idea of moving from employer to employer. Workers became less hesitant to jump ship in order to enhance their careers (or their potential compensation packages). Senior-level workers moved with more frequency into the new "click-and-mortar" jobs, and traditional corporations were faced with filling vacancies left in their wake. Enter the executive search firm into a market created by demand.

Executive recruiting works for other reasons as well:

☼ In addition to networking (which we'll talk about in chapter 5), executive recruiting is an easy way to find jobs that may not be advertised. Executive recruiters are also much more adept at mining the ever-growing Internet

A Recruiting Renaissance

Recruiting reached its heyday at the turn of the twenty-first century before a slowing economy led to a prolonged downturn. Today recruiting is on the rebound. In 2004, most of the top twenty-five recruiting firms in the United States reported double-digit increases in revenue—and the top firm, Korn/Ferry International, saw its revenue approach a half-billion dollars. Current events have also played a role in the renaissance of executive recruiting, as outrage over scandals has created more turnover at the top of the corporate food chain.

landscape for available positions you may have a hard time finding on your own due to time constraints.

☼ Executive search firms provide a higher degree of confidentiality than going it alone for candidates who want to keep their search under wraps from their present employers.

☼ Recruiters create a buffer between a corporation and a potentially long list of executive aspirants, while at the same time giving those same applicants a longer list of potential employers from which to choose.

☼ Working with an executive recruiter builds a continuing relationship between those searching for work and those with an inside track on where the jobs are. Remember: You'll probably be looking for work again at some point in the future.

Because employers pay the recruiter's fee (typically about one-third of the successful candidate's starting annual salary), placements are carefully considered. The recruiter-employer relationship is critically important, and this works to your advantage. Recruiters are extremely selective about which candidates to present as possible hires; if you're deemed to be one of them, you can be confident that a lot of vetting was involved in the process.

Hefty fees work in your favor as well. A recruiter will not risk upsetting his corporate client by placing a mediocre candidate in a high-paying position. The recruiter's fee for filling a $180,000 position could be in the neighborhood of $60,000. However, the cost of a bad hire at this level is much greater than just the fee paid to a recruiter. A bad hire can damage an employer's reputation (as well as a recruiter's), decrease morale among employees, adversely affect a company's position in the marketplace, damage relationships between the employer and its suppliers, and much more.

take a memo

A Word of Caution

Avoid submitting unsolicited resumes to executive recruiters. It's a waste of time, because rarely will it result in a job match. The best you can hope for is that your basic information (industry, job title, salary range, and so forth) will be entered into a "futures" database in the event that a position matching your qualifications becomes available. More likely, you'll receive a call from the recruiter to see if you know of any possible candidates for a position you're not suited for yourself.

After all, recruiters also know the value of networking.

MATCHMAKER, MATCHMAKER, MAKE ME A MATCH

By now, you may be asking yourself, "How do I get an executive recruiter of my very own?" To paraphrase an ancient proverb: You do not find him. He finds you.

As we just mentioned, today's recruiter is deluged with unsolicited resumes. Most of these will receive only a cursory glance before being tossed aside. In fact, one recruiter we spoke to estimates that he receives more than ten thousand unsolicited resumes a year and, in most years, *not a single one* of those resumes results in a placement. Clearly, you do not want to go this route.

If recruiters aren't contacting you, you need to grab their attention. The most effective way to do this is simply to become better known in your field. As your visibility increases, your chances of attracting the interest of a recruiter will increase as well.

To increase your visibility, try some of the strategies we list on pages 37–38. In addition to gaining the attention of executive recruiters, many of these tactics may get you noticed by key decision makers in your current organization, if you're presently employed. We'll explore the topic of self-promotion more fully in chapter 4.

Your Action	Possible Result
Publish papers in an industry trade magazine.	Good recruiters are very knowledge-able about the industry. Your name atop an impressive article could be all it takes to get you noticed.
Speak at conferences or, at the very least, take part in panel discussions.	While a recruiter may not attend the conference, it won't hurt to have your name (and, along with it, your biogra-phy and qualifications) listed on the conference Web site and printed materials handed out to conference attendees.
Make yourself available to local/national media as a source of information in your industry.	This is free publicity! Plus, you may be surprised at how quickly your name becomes identified with your field of work. Media outlets have launched entire careers for "experts" who were unknown until they were tapped over and over again as "knowledgeable sources" about their industries. Think about it: Had you ever heard of Dr. Sanjay Gupta before CNN made him a star?
Diversify yourself by broadening your skills base.	CEOs (even corporate VPs) wear many hats and respond to a variety of shareholder concerns. Prove that you are capable of handling everything thrown at you. If your entire career has been in sales, try your hand at marketing. If you've spent many years in operations, it wouldn't hurt to add budgeting to your skills.

Your Action	Possible Result
Increase your network of professional colleagues.	Word of mouth goes a long way in helping a recruiter find you. Recruiters are in the people business, and they have a wide range of contacts. If your name keeps popping up in their conversations, you'll have no trouble attracting one.
Join every professional organization for which you qualify—and take a leadership role in one or two of them.	This works for many of the reasons already specified above. As a plus, it also shows that you are passionate about (or at least dedicated to) your field, and concerned about the possible direction in which it is headed. The key: Don't just join. Lead.
Self-promote.	Many people have a hard time with this concept, no doubt as a result of no-nonsense upbringings aimed at ensuring humility. Blame your parents later. For now, recognize that it's okay to blow your own horn, as long as you can back it up.

THE RELATIONSHIP BEGINS

So you've taken all the advice above and, lo and behold, a recruiter has contacted you. If you're lucky, perhaps several have contacted you. What next?

An introductory phone call is the first step, hopefully followed by a chance to meet. First impressions are important on both sides. The phone call only assesses your qualifications, and its intention is to determine whether a meeting should even take place. There's a chance that either one of you may decide the time isn't right, or you simply don't "click" for whatever reason.

On the other hand, if the phone call goes well, the face-to-face meeting is when the relationship truly begins.

You and the recruiter will both want to project your best possible image. For the recruiter, this is the easy part. She is accustomed to meeting potential new candidates and instilling confidence and trust in them. This may not be as easy for you, but it is vital for you to inspire in her the same level of confidence and trust.

During your first meeting, you will face a series of questions designed to determine your viability as a potential candidate for openings the recruiter is already trying to fill. There's also a chance you'll be screened for placement in a pool of candidates, readily available for contact at some point in the future.

PREPARING FOR YOUR MEETING

We'll discuss interviewing in detail in chapter 7. In addition, entire books are dedicated to preparing for a job interview. They can offer you some assistance, particularly if it's been several years since you last interviewed. A list of valuable resources on the interviewing process appears at the end of chapter 7. In the meantime, here are some important pointers for interviewing with executive recruiters.

Be Honest at All Times

Leadership is about integrity and honesty, particularly in the wake of recent scandals at companies like Enron and Tyco. If you're asked about your current compensation, give an accurate account. Stifle the urge to inflate your salary in order to attract a higher offer. Always assume your salary information is discoverable, even if you consider it a carefully guarded personal detail to which few are privy. Using deceit to pad a potential offer is not worth the risk of killing your relationship with the recruiter.

Be Forthcoming

Know the difference between reasons and excuses. Reasons explain why something happened despite your best efforts. Excuses tend to place blame somewhere else while "exonerating" you. Even if you're 100 percent correct in your assessment, excuses will portray you as the antithesis of a stand-up individual—which, of course, is one of the primary character traits we demand of our leaders.

Expect a Challenge

You'll be interviewing for a high-level position, so you should anticipate some pretty stringent questioning. You may find some of the questions difficult to answer; that's exactly why these questions are being asked in the first place.

Approach each question head-on and don't get defensive. In particular, practice your answers to the following questions:

- ☼ What was your biggest challenge and how did you handle it?
- ☼ How would you describe your most successful moment?
- ☼ What has been your greatest failure so far and how did you recover from it?
- ☼ Thinking back on previous workplace failures, what did you learn about yourself?
- ☼ What are your worst traits, and how do you handle them?
- ☼ What are your visions for this industry?
- ☼ What is your workplace philosophy?
- ☼ What is it about this position that appeals to you?
- ☼ In your current position, what recognition have you received?

Finally, ask yourself: What is the worst possible question I could imagine being asked? Then come up with an answer for it. In addition, be prepared for background checks, credit checks, close scrutiny of your references and your resume, proof that you added to the company's profitability in previous positions, and (if you've gotten through all this) call-back interviews that may or may not involve corporate representatives.

Keep It Professional

Meeting the recruiter is nearly the same as meeting the employer—or, in some cases, the board of directors for every company the recruiter represents. Do not make the mistake of acting too "chummy" with him. The nature of his work forces a recruiter not only to remain neutral, but also to relay any and all information about you to the employer. This includes his impression of how you conduct yourself in a setting that is both professional and social at the same time.

QUESTIONS YOU SHOULD ASK

You've prepared yourself for the questions you'll face; it's also important to come to the meeting with questions of your own. Here are some valid questions we suggest asking:

☼ **Which industries do you represent? Which companies?** Just because the recruiter thinks you may be a potential fit somewhere doesn't make it so. By now, you know enough about your industry to determine if this particular recruiter has enough experience in your field to help advance your career.

☼ **What can you tell me about your client(s)?** Be wary of vague answers. For each company the recruiter represents, ask about the corporate culture, most recent financial information, future plans—almost anything should be fair game. Remember: If the recruiter has a specific position in mind for you, you've already been vetted. You have a right to as much information as you can possibly get. He's certainly trying to get everything he can from you.

☼ **How many executives have you placed in the past? With these clients? At which levels?** The answers to these questions give you a sense of the recruiter's past performance. Ask for references while you're at it, because you're going to be asked to provide yours. Your relationship with a recruiter will be a partnership; in a partnership, the qualifications of both parties are validated.

☼ **What made you contact me?** This is perhaps the most important question you can ask, because the answer will tell you where your strengths lie and give you a clue as to achievements you can highlight in future interviews.

☼ **Can you provide details about the position?** Again, watch for vague responses. Ask whether this is a new position, or whether you are replacing someone who has left the company. If you're replacing someone, why did she leave? What are the measurable expectations for the job (i.e., number of new product launches, profitability projections, expansion goals)?

☼ **With whom do you have contact in the organization?** The higher-level the recruiter's contact, the better, as far as you're concerned. A recruiter who answers to the human resources department is not as valuable to you as one who has an "in" with the board of directors or the CEO/CFO.

☼ **Is there a written job description?** If not, ask for one.

Remember to ask all your questions in the most diplomatic way possible. It will not do you much good to come across as abrasive or offensive. (Again, think about that "small world" that we talked about at the end of chapter 1.)

Do *not* ask questions that could have been answered with a little bit of research on your part. For example, if you knew in advance that you were going to be screened for a vice-presidency at Widgets, Inc., don't ask about quarterly earnings; instead, track down this information in advance. Not only will it give you a better idea of the company's viability, but—with a well-placed reference to the data during your conversation—you'll come across as someone seriously interested in moving ahead.

NURTURING THE RELATIONSHIP

After the interview, the recruiter will have a better feel for you as a candidate. You should have a better feel for the recruiter as well. If the position for which the recruiter is considering you isn't right, or you leave the meeting without total confidence in the recruiter's abilities and past performance, don't be afraid to end the relationship. Keep in mind that you are the commodity being sought; you didn't go searching for anything. Trust us: If one recruiter found you, others will, too. Be patient.

On the other hand, hopefully things went quite well during your face-to-face interview. In that case, you now have your very own, bona fide executive recruiter. This will certainly increase your opportunities for advancement—if not now, then at some point down the line.

It's the start of a beautiful relationship. After placing you with a new employer, a savvy recruiter will keep close tabs on your career (and may return with a more lucrative opportunity a couple of years later).

For example, an executive recruiter helped Rosemary, a native of the UK, find a job she loved while she was living in London. A short time later, she relocated to New York to accept another position within the company. When her firm's chief competitor made a foray into the European market, Rosemary's regular correspondence with the recruiter planted her foremost in his mind when he received the assignment to staff the new office. As it turned out, Rosemary was ready to return to her homeland. Her ongoing relationship with the recruiter gave her the opportunity to do so.

Even if you aren't thinking about moving on, you'd be wise to maintain your relationship with the recruiter. The longer you remain with your new employer, the more entrenched your recruiter will feel in your company's hiring process. Placing you could lead to dozens of additional placements for him. And he'll show his gratitude to you by putting you at the top of his list for new positions that open up in the executive suite.

You and the executive recruiter each have the potential to help the other now and in the future, perhaps multiple times. It's a win-win relationship for both of you—one you should enjoy and benefit from. In the next chapter, we'll discuss other means of discovering—and creating—important opportunities to advance your career.

Recommended Books

Be Hunted!: 12 Secrets to Getting on the Headhunter's Radar Screen by Smooch S. Reynolds (John Wiley & Sons, 2001, ISBN 0471410748, $19.95).

The Directory of Executive Recruiters 2005 (Kennedy Information, 2004, ISBN 1932079335, $49.95).

Headhunters Revealed! Career Secrets for Choosing and Using Professional Recruiters by Darrell W. Gurney (Hunter Arts, 2001, ISBN 0967422906, $14.95).

Kennedy's Pocket Guide to Working with Executive Recruiters (Kennedy Publications, 2002, ISBN 1885922388, $17.95).

Navigating Your Career: 21 of America's Leading Headhunters Tell You How It's Done by Christopher W. Hunt (John Wiley & Sons, 1998, ISBN 0471254347, $19.95).

The Road to CEO: The World's Leading Executive Recruiters Identify the Traits You Need to Make It to the Top by Sharon Voros (Adams Media, 2002, ISBN 1580627099, $10.95).

Recommended Web Sites

The Recruiter's Studio—Hosted by recruiter Cheryl Ferguson:
http://www.therecruitersstudio.com

BlueSteps—Service of the Association of Executive Search Consultants:
http://www.bluesteps.com

Executive Registry—Members may search jobs from executive recruiters:
http://www.executiveregistry.com

6FigureJobs.com—Online executive career portal:
http://www.6figurejobs.com

CHAPTER 4

Blatant Self-Promotion...
on the Sly

"First of all—you need a Web site."

In the previous chapter, we discussed the pivotal role an executive recruiter can play as you advance your career. It's great if you've got one (or more) working to help you move ahead. But what if you haven't shown up on a recruiter's radar screen yet? What if you don't even *need* a recruiter, because you're confident that your current company is teeming with opportunities?

What if you need to create opportunities for yourself?

Recruiters can be invaluable in connecting you with your next post, but the job of creating opportunities and making a name for yourself falls squarely on you. If you're adept at doing so, the route to the corner office should be much smoother and, perhaps, a bit shorter in length.

Imagine yourself as an aspiring professional athlete hoping to sign a big-money contract. In order to get the best possible deal, you'll need an agent—but he can only help you after you demonstrate that you have the tools to succeed in the league. In fact, he won't even take you on as a client until you do so. Without size, speed, and talent, you're unmarketable.

In other words, the first move toward an executive assignment is yours. To succeed, you must make yourself more marketable.

Brand Yourself

It's time to get your name into heavy circulation inside and outside the company. Become a well-known commodity. Brand yourself. It's easier than you think; it just requires initiative and time on your part.

Self-promotion is an art unto itself, and, just as in the art world, there are many tools you can use and different ways in which you can use them. One tool of particular importance is the media. The beauty of the media is that learning how to use it—and, ultimately, master it—doesn't have to cost you a dime. A word of caution, however: If you're currently employed, before availing yourself of any media, clear it with your company's media relations department. This is particularly important in larger corporations, in which official spokespeople are the only ones authorized to speak as company representatives, and specific policies prohibit "rogue" interviews. Your first step into the world of public relations shouldn't land on the toes of your CEO.

Start Small

Unless you've stumbled onto something extremely compelling (like corporate corruption), put off any grandiose ideas about seeing your name in the *Wall Street Journal*. It's not going to happen—yet. Your initial concern is to appear in any publication. Write a column for your company newsletter. Contact the editor of a trade publication and ask if the publication accepts submitted articles in your area of expertise. Write a letter to the editor of the local newspaper. If your letter concerns an issue that (based on your current position) you're qualified to speak on, enhance the free publicity by including your job title and company name underneath your name (once you've cleared it with your corporate PR department).

The writing isn't your goal. The *reading* is. The more times you are published, the more opportunities people have to see your name tied to your industry. Some of these people will be executive recruiters, upper-management types, and leaders at your firm's competitors.

For example, in the pre-Web days of the early '90s, Bill worked for a small dialup gaming service that included fantasy sports games as one of its components. As an extra offering to the company's customers (who only numbered a few thousand), he started writing weekly "insider tips" columns for those who played the games: which pitchers were scheduled to pitch twice each week, which hitters were hot, and which ones were suffering through prolonged slumps.

Bill wrote his columns on his own time for no extra money. However, shortly after he began writing, his work attracted the interest of a newspaper chain, which agreed to syndicate his column to its papers across the country. Within two years, Bill was serving as the featured guest on coast-to-coast radio interviews and writing preseason forecasts for national publications.

And it all came about by starting small.

Broaden Your Exposure

By following the suggestions for starting small, you've begun the process of self-promotion. Self-promotion can be uncomfortable for many people; however, you'll find it's a necessity. If you aspire to be a corporate leader, commit the following truth to memory—and repeat it as frequently as possible:

Carefully considered self-promotion is essential during your rise to the top.

Taylor, a sales account manager in Chicago, discovered this the hard way. The "chest beaters" within her company were a constant source of irritation to her. Especially frustrating was seeing these same people regularly promoted ahead of her. Eventually, she realized that she would need to get over her fear of appearing self-aggrandizing if she wanted to get ahead. Wary of approaching her boss directly to spell out her accomplishments, she began utilizing a tool at her disposal—the internal company blog site—to highlight her achievements and maintain an informal dialogue with colleagues. It worked: Taylor soon found herself being considered for high-level promotions, and eventually received one.

Self-promotion is nothing more than public relations on a very small scale. You're simply marketing yourself to a targeted audience instead of marketing a product to the masses. Keep in mind that, unlike the masses, members of your target audience—including your supervisors, industry leaders, and executive recruiters—are quite shrewd. If you cross the line from "carefully considered PR" to "shameless self-promotion," they will see right through it.

What's next? Well, you can't keep writing letters to the editor forever. Continuing to publish on a regular basis is a good idea, but you can still increase your exposure. If you're in a position to do so, work with your PR department to send out press releases. Use these to announce promotions, congratulate your staff members for achieving significant professional milestones, publicize a recent award, or explain your company's (or your division's) foray into a new area of business. Be sure to drop in a quote of your own, so your name and title figure prominently in these press releases.

If you're with a small business that lacks a PR team, the business section of your local newspaper may be a great place to start. They will gladly run news items based on your press releases, provided they are relevant and well written. They may even decide to write a feature piece about you. Here's why:

1. Newsprint costs remain high, and newspapers are constantly looking for ways to trim this cost.

2. Business sections are getting leaner, most often by trimming the stock listings. Most investors track their portfolios online with real-time quotes, rendering newspaper listings irrelevant.

3. While the trimming of stock quotes has aided in the thinning of business sections, they remain stand-alone sections in most metropolitan newspapers. As a result, many papers are faced with a larger local "news hole" in the business section—even with a reduced page count.

4. A larger local business news hole requires more local business news, which, in turn, generates more reader interest (and boosts circulation).

Other career moves accomplish the same goals without appearing blatantly self-promotional. While they don't necessarily involve the media, the potential payoff in terms of exposure makes them worth considering:

☼ **Activity:** Teach a course at a local college or community center.

Possible Payoffs: Looks great on a resume. Plus, it qualifies you as an expert on the topic at hand while providing real-life experience as a public speaker. In the short term you have nothing to lose in this endeavor, but the long-term benefits could be priceless.

Anecdotal Support: Current Secretary of Energy Sam Bodman began his career as an associate professor. From there, he eventually became chief operating officer of Fidelity Investments. We're not suggesting that his professorship led to his rise to COO or a U.S. Cabinet position, but those six years of teaching certainly must have honed his speaking skills.

☼ **Activity:** Take part in a panel discussion at a professional seminar.

Possible Payoffs: Not everyone can be the keynote speaker, but trade shows and other large gatherings offer plenty of other high-visibility opportunities that can provide essentially the same payoff, with much lower risk. Being a panelist is a good first step if you have never spoken at a conference before: You'll get a taste of what it's like to be the center of attention while having a chance to pass on a question or ask another panel member for her thoughts, in case you can't come up with an answer right away.

Anecdotal Support: You (or, more accurately, your name) will live on far longer than the discussion itself—in perpetuity, thanks to the Web. Want proof? A Yahoo! search on the combined terms *health care, conference, transcript*, and *panelist* returned thousands of hits—some from conferences that were eight to ten years old. Information about panel members was included in most of the articles. Talk about long-lasting publicity!

☼ **Activity:** Give a speech at a conference.

Possible Payoffs: In a roomful of industry insiders, everyone's attention will be on you *and only you*. Plus, your name will be listed in the handouts and daily agendas for the conference—something top recruiters tend to get their hands on when searching for new talent. To take full advantage of this opportunity, you must recognize that, to most conference attendees, one speaker is indistinguishable from another. Find a way to stand out. Don't think of it as a speech, but rather as a show. Give it some life. Your listeners will not only thank you for it, they'll remember who you are. One caveat: This is a high-risk, high-reward activity. Don't try it unless you know you can nail it. Success on the dais can launch you higher on the corporate ladder, but struggling in public could hinder your aspirations.

Anecdotal Support: Two words—Barack Obama. If you're a little fuzzy on the name, think back to the 2004 Democratic National Convention. Obama, a political unknown, was inexplicably tapped as the keynote speaker at the convention. His speech drew rave reviews from most political pundits, some of whom rated it more effective than former President Clinton's speech during the same convention. Result: Obama, coming off a failed attempt for a U.S. congressional seat four years earlier, won election to the U.S. Senate that November.

☼ **Activity:** Take a leadership role in a trade association.

Possible Payoffs: Having group ties within your industry is a very useful networking resource, and we'll talk more about networking in the next chapter. By taking a leadership role in one of these organizations, you'll be able to quietly ride the coattails of the group to increase your own visibility. You'll also increase your chances of landing other public speaking gigs and making valuable media contacts.

Anecdotal Support: As a newspaper copyeditor, Tammy wasn't in a position to comment publicly as a spokeswoman for her employer. However, membership in a national copyeditors' association led to a seat on its executive board, allowing her to learn about job openings at newspapers across the country and positioning her as an industry expert through various public speaking engagements arranged through the association.

Become a Media Darling

At this point, you've established yourself as an authority on a certain topic or range of topics. Savvy media insiders—including news producers or reporters who cover your industry—will have already found their way to your doorstep. Those who haven't may need a little bit of help. Offer your services. A well-crafted letter to the managing editor of the local newspaper and the directors of news operations at television network affiliates (and local talk-radio stations) may be all it takes to get your name placed in their "source" files. Again, if you're currently employed, clear this in advance with the appropriate people within your company.

Survey the landscape! Find the fit that allows you to give an expert opinion. Let's say you live in a geographic region undergoing significant population growth. Urban sprawl and rapid suburban development, therefore, are primary challenges. Guess who's qualified to offer input to the media: public works employees, realtors, developers, banking officials, architects, traffic engineers, public safety officials, educational leaders, and small business owners—just to name a few.

Pretend, for a moment, that you're a traffic engineer. In the above scenario, your letter to local media, in which you offer your services as a source of information, could include the following qualifications:

As development in our region continues, careful thought needs to be given to which areas can sustain various types of housing—from million-dollar, single-family homes to large apartment complexes. I have spent the past ten years studying and improving local traffic patterns. In addition, I am familiar with the long-range planning of city leaders, allowing me to recognize potential problems well in advance of any construction.

Given all that, which local news organization wouldn't solicit your input whenever a new housing development was being proposed?

Don't fret too much that you're not the "best" source in your field. You don't have to be. You just have to be knowledgeable, engaging, and reliable. The nature of the news cycle frequently forces reporters to call at strange hours. For that reason, when you offer your services as an expert source, be sure to provide multiple contact numbers (including office, home, and cell phone numbers). Answer the call every time, provide a response for every question, and be as personable as possible.

Reporters are always on the lookout for more sources to help them flesh out their stories, and they're extremely reluctant to throw away any source at all. Given a choice between calling a rarely available source or one who is helpful and easily accessible, reporters facing a deadline will choose the latter every time.

Camera-Conscious and Microphone-Friendly

Now it's time to polish your public image. If you've been successful at self-promotion up to this point, your profile (locally and perhaps nationally) has been dramatically heightened. Hopefully, people will now want to put a face with your name, and producers in the largest of all media—television—will help them do that by parading you in front of the public to speak knowingly about Topic X whenever they need an expert opinion. Again, leave your self-doubts behind.

You don't have to be the very best at what you do at this point, but you'd better be very good. If you can give the public a sense that you can be trusted implicitly, you'll essentially create the demand for your services. It's a wonderful, never-ending cycle that continually enhances your reputation (which is why you started the process in the first place). Seriously, does anyone really think Dr. Phil is the best psychiatrist in America?

Of course, the odds are that you will not become a TV or radio personality. There are plenty of industries that receive little or no on-air media coverage. No problem. You're still going to get increased exposure in outlets like trade publications, training seminars, and industry conferences. Which means you need to make the camera (and the tape recorder) your friend:

☼ **Pay careful attention to your appearance.** Studies have shown that attractive people tend to earn more money than their less-striking counterparts. A 2001 University of Texas study claims "good-looking" professionals enjoy a 12 percent advantage in pay over less attractive people. If you are carrying a few extra pounds, you may want to consider whether an exercise regimen could give you an edge as you plot your future. In addition to improving your appearance, maintaining a healthy weight can also boost your workplace morale: According to a 2005 study by employee assistance provider ComPsych, 22 percent of very overweight employees suffered from low morale, almost twice the percentage as healthy-weight employees.

☼ **Dress for success.** The adage "Don't dress for the job you have, dress for the job you want" has been around forever. But it's surprising how infrequently it's heeded, particularly in offices where the dress code slants toward "working casual." If you have any doubt about how you should dress, err on the side of caution. It's better to be overdressed than underdressed. Here's another idea: Check out how your current CEO dresses. After all, it's his job (or one like it) that you're interested in winning.

☼ **Learn to talk in sound bites.** Whether you're being interviewed or giving a speech, try to speak in eight- to ten-second phrases capable of standing on their own. Because, chances are, they'll have to. Due to time constraints, the producers editing the tape (or the reporter writing the article) won't be able to use most of what you say. Phrase your thoughts in "nuggets," or easily digestible bites.

Be Web-Savvy

Finally, consider making yourself visible on the Web. You can accomplish this by writing pieces for online magazines or streaming a prerecorded copy of one of your more impressive speeches on an industry—or your company's—Web site. Consider starting your own blog; however, as we previously mentioned, only include information you'd feel comfortable sharing with your current or future employer.

The internet offers valuable opportunities to increase your exposure and gain the attention of decision makers in your industry and your organization. Do whatever you can to fully take advantage of this medium—whether that includes hiring a professional to assist you or learning the skills you need to make use of this technology.

BREAK OUT OF THE PACK: RISING TO THE TOP WHERE YOU ARE

If you're looking to advance in your current company, you're going to need to outshine your competitors—in this case, your colleagues. Outside of the political world, no one is going to champion someone else for a promotion. Even though your workplace may be filled with office politics, it's certainly not an environment where your peers will nominate you as a possible candidate to become the Next Great Leader. They're too busy positioning themselves for that honor. Clearly, if you want to get ahead, you need to enter the fray all on your own.

That's a pretty easy task for those extroverted, sociable souls who network with ease and view each office relationship in terms of *Can this person help me advance?* Yet in any company, there are dozens of highly qualified individuals, fully capable of assuming leadership, who simply aren't comfortable with the idea of using who they know as a means to get something that should be based on what they know.

We call these individuals "nice people." You may even be one of them. It's perfectly okay, even desirable, to be nice. After all, virtually all our parents raised us to "play nice." But at some point, winning becomes a priority. We're told that being nice and winning don't go hand in hand.

But nice guys don't always finish last; in many cases, nice guys actually get things done very efficiently. Their treatment of subordinates inspires a loyalty and a do-or-die attitude that proves invaluable. The reality is that you *can* be nice and still win; however, if you're overly nice, others may exploit this "weakness" as they pass you by on their way to the top.

take a memo

Give 'Em Hell, Shrinking Violets!

It's important to remember that not all "wallflowers" end up missing out on the big dance. Tales of reluctant leaders are scattered throughout history. Perhaps the best-known example in America is that of Harry S. Truman, the thirty-third president of the United States. During the 1944 Democratic National Convention, Truman—a one-time Missouri business-man who had been on the brink of bankruptcy near the age of forty and had narrowly won reelection to the U.S. Senate four years earlier—had to be talked into accepting the vice presidential nomination.

The reason? The failing health of popular president Franklin Delano Roosevelt made it very likely that whoever was chosen as his running mate would wind up finishing Roosevelt's fourth term. Truman, who freely admitted to being a "sissy" growing up, wanted no part of that challenge.

Yet Truman eventually agreed to the nomination; eighty-two days into FDR's fourth term, Roosevelt died and the unassuming Missourian became president. Less than four months later, he faced what is (even today) perhaps the biggest decision ever confronted by one man in the history of this planet: whether to use atomic bombs to hasten the end of World War II.

▶**Action Items: Are You Nice, or Too Nice?**

Think about your current work environment. Which of the following statements would you agree with?

- ☼ Coworkers sometimes ask for my help because they know I have a hard time saying no.

- ☼ I choose to avoid conflict whenever possible.

- ☼ I have never disputed a statement on my performance evaluation.

- ☼ My supervisors do not have a good idea of what my goals are.

- ☼ My pay raise seems to be about the same every year no matter how well I do my job.

- ☼ I don't have time for things I like to do.

☼ I am concerned about how other people think of me.

If you recognize yourself in two or more of those statements, you're not being nice; you're being overly nice. It's time to take a stand—for you!

☼ Don't be ashamed to say no to a colleague's request for help.

☼ Recognize that not all conflict is avoidable.

☼ Pleasing everyone is impossible—so stop trying to do so.

☼ If you truly believe that your performance evaluation is inaccurate or does not take into account something it should, mention it!

☼ Tactfully discuss your career aspirations with those around you.

The bottom line here is simply this: If you deal with everyone in as straightforward a manner as possible, avoid a reputation as a corporate doormat, and demonstrate that you have a clear vision of what your future holds, you'll develop a "nice-guy" reputation while at the same time instilling confidence in your peers and your superiors. And that can be a big marker on the table when office promotions are being discussed.

Facing a Crisis

Opportunities aren't always created. Neither do they exist only in favorable situations. Sometimes, they arise out of the most trying of circumstances. Pessimists call them obstacles. Leaders see them as challenges to overcome. Take a look at how each of the following crises was handled, and the end result of each:

☼ Former New York City Mayor Rudy Giuliani is widely regarded in retrospect as the person who may have done more than anyone—including President Bush—to soothe American fears in the days and weeks after the terrorist attacks of September 11, 2001. His confident demeanor and businesslike determination that the city could, and would, overcome an unfathomable catastrophe was exactly what the nation needed to see. As a result, Giuliani (whose approval rating had fallen below 40 percent before the attacks) is now mentioned as the Republican Party's possible 2008 presidential nominee—and some early polls show he would defeat top Democratic candidates.

☼ In the confusion that followed John Hinckley's assassination attempt of President Reagan in 1981, Secretary of State Alexander Haig

THINK Outside the Box

Manage Your Boss

It's not uncommon for an employee's performance evaluation to be substantially inaccurate; yet many workers don't voice their objections to these yearly reviews, despite their impact on future appraisals. Treat your evaluations just as you would treat your credit report: Challenge anything you don't agree with. If your supervisors don't have solid evidence to support the statements made in the review, insist that the review be amended.

Before you meet with your boss to discuss your points of contention, consider how you will present your argument. Be objective. See where you are in agreement with her—even if a comment is negative—and think about how you can improve your performance in that area. Identifying common ground may prevent your supervisor from becoming defensive. You'll then be in a better position to challenge other parts of the evaluation. Be ready to back up your claims with hard, uncontestable facts, and never challenge the evaluation in the same meeting in which you're first seeing it. Ask for time to look it over before you discuss it.

appeared before reporters (and a national television audience) to answer questions. When asked who was in charge, Haig famously responded, "I'm in charge here"—completely forgetting about the line of succession provided for in the U.S. Constitution. While his intentions may have been good, Haig was quickly portrayed as a power-monger and crucified in the press. He resigned the following year.

Remember: *Anyone* can be a successful leader in an optimal situation. Phil Jackson has won eight NBA titles, and many observers regard him as one of the best coaches in basketball history. But Jackson had the good fortune to coach two of the game's all-time great players: Michael Jordan (with whom Jackson won six championships while with the Chicago Bulls) and Shaquille O'Neal (who helped Jackson win back-to-back titles with the Los Angeles Lakers). Jackson left each team at the same time that his marquee player moved on. Was Jackson a great coach or simply a fortunate one? The only way to determine that is to see how he fares in the future without the services of a superlative player.

Problems crop up in your workplace on a near-daily basis. Most never make it onto the radar screen of upper management, because people like you are expected to handle them and make things right. However, every once in a while a real catastrophe strikes. Your company may plan for a wide range of contingencies, but a dire situation that no one could have predicted is almost certain to arise at some point. On those occasions, upper management may have no idea who to turn to.

Sometimes, in the most trying of circumstances, unexpected leaders emerge and restore order to a chaotic situation. Be one of those people. If you can handle the problem properly, you can establish a reputation among your supervisors as a cool-headed, confident leader.

In the next chapter, we'll talk exclusively about another important tool you can use to find vacancies without the aid of a recruiter: your personal network of friends, friends of friends, colleagues, and pretty much everyone you meet from this point on.

RECOMMENDED BOOKS

Be Your Own Brand: A Breakthrough Formula for Standing Out from the Crowd by David McNally and Karl D. Speak (Berrett-Koehler, 2003, ISBN 1576752720, $14.95).

The Brand You 50: Fifty Ways to Transform Yourself from an "Employee" into a Brand That Shouts Distinction, Commitment, and Passion! by Tom Peters (Knopf, 1999, ISBN 0375407723, $15.95).

Brand Yourself: How to Create an Identity for a Brilliant Career by David Andrusia (Ballantine Books, 1999, ISBN 0345423593, $14.00).

Career Warfare: 10 Rules for Building a Successful Personal Brand and Fighting to Keep It by David F. D'Alessandro (McGraw-Hill, 2004, ISBN 0071417583, $21.95).

Confidence: How Winning Streaks & Losing Streaks Begin and End by Rosabeth Moss Kanter (Crown Publishing Group, 2004, ISBN 1400052904, $27.50).

Creating You & Co.: Learn to Think Like the CEO of Your Own Career by William Bridges (Perseus Books, 1998, ISBN 0738200328, $16.50).

The Five Patterns of Extraordinary Careers: The Guide for Achieving Success and Satisfaction, by James M. Citrin & Richard A. Smith (Crown Publishing Group, 2003, ISBN 1400047943, $22.95).

Make a Name for Yourself: Eight Steps for Creating an Unforgettable Personal Brand Strategy for Success by Robin Fisher Roffer (Broadway Books, 2002, ISBN 0767904923, $14.00).

Promoting Yourself: 52 Lessons for Getting to the Top—and Staying There by Hal Lancaster (Free Press, 2004, ISBN 0743213645, $12.00).

RECOMMENDED WEB SITES

10 Tips for Marketing Yourself and Your Business—by Rob Engleman, Engleman Management Group:
http://www.pertinent.com/articles/marketing/engelmanM1.asp

ExecuNet—Executive Job Search, Networking & Career Advancement:
http://www.execunet.com

ExecutivesOnly—Prescreened executive jobs:
http://www.executivesonly.com

RiteSite.com—Executive career information exchange:
http://www.ritesite.com

CHAPTER 5

Fine-Tuning
Your Network:
It's *Who* You Know

"Last week it was all communications people. Lord knows what group we're networking with today."

T hink about all the job offers you've received in the past. Not just the ones you accepted, but also the offers you turned down, regardless of the reason.

How many of those were jobs you truly won on your own, with no assistance from a friend, relative, former coworker, or other helpful acquaintance? How many offers have you attracted without the aid of someone who had an "in" within the hiring process?

If you're like most American workers, you've probably had some help along the way. The old axiom—"It's not what you know, it's who you know"—rings truer than you might think. This is why *networking*—interweaving all the people you know—is considered such a vital component in career success.

We realize this all sounds familiar to you; you've likely relied on networking to get to this point in your career. But does the importance of networking fade as you climb the corporate ladder? After all, it's one thing for the father of your best friend to put in a good word for you when you're aspiring to an entry-level (or even mid-level) position. What happens at the executive level?

Networking at this point remains a valuable asset. Your contacts can be extremely helpful in determining where the jobs are and putting you in touch with the right people. In this chapter, we will explore some steps you can take to ensure that your network is growing and that you're doing your part to help it thrive. At the same time, you should consider weeding through it periodically— and we'll give you some tips on how to do that as well. Finally, we'll help you uncover already existing networks you should consider adding to your portfolio of contacts.

QUALITY VERSUS QUANTITY

In chapter 3, we discussed the hesitancy some job seekers have in using the services of an executive search firm. Likewise, many are reluctant to turn to net-working during the hunt for work—because, unfortunately, most people don't know how to network properly. They approach the process in the same way they did when they were first starting out, focusing primarily on generating contacts.

Think about it. Networking for entry-level employees is solely about numbers: How many people do I know? How many people *can* I know? How many business cards can I distribute? Which of my friends will introduce me to all their friends? How many potential customers can I meet? What can these people do for me?

This is not a bad way to live—when you're twenty-five. Life isn't so much about quality as it is about quantity. You measure your opportunities in sheer numbers, because sheer numbers ensure a certain measure of success. To be sure, some contacts are more valuable than others, but, in the early stages of their careers, most young professionals aren't very discriminating about who becomes part of their career network.

It's analogous to telemarketing: If you make five hundred calls a day and are unsuccessful 99 percent of the time, you've still made five sales, which may not be a bad day's work. In this example, your network is measured by *how many* contacts you have, not the *value* of each individual contact.

But you're not twenty-five anymore. Networking isn't merely about contacts; it's about your relationships with *specific* contacts. Unlike the connections you've built in the past, your executive network should be somewhat discriminating.

Hopefully, your networking skills have evolved during your rise toward the top—from the scattershot method you used when you were clawing your way up from the bottom rungs to a much more focused approach. If you're still networking the old way, it's time to refine your methods. In upper management, the question you should be asking isn't, "What can *you* do for *me*?" To network effectively at this level, you need to shift the question to, "What can *we* do for *each other*?"

DARWINISM AT WORK

If you're worried that your network is full of contacts and short on relationships, spend some time separating the wheat from the chaff. Business hierarchies, like all hierarchies, tend to be shaped like pyramids, so it's time to recognize that there are fewer people available who can truly help you as you move up the food chain. Fewer people work at or near the top of the business model; logically, it follows that fewer people can actually help place you in a leadership position.

For that reason, take a long look at those people you consider to be current members of your network and thin the herd. Go through your Rolodex or contact list and honestly assess the value of each person as a source for professional advancement. If you can't envision how a contact might help you get where you want to be, he or she probably can't.

Some of the "expendables" will be friends and other contacts you genuinely want to keep in touch with for a myriad of reasons. But if they can't realistically help you into the corner office, move them out of your *professional* network.

You've just done something completely implausible, at least according to typical networking protocol: You've decreased (perhaps significantly) your number of contacts. Was this career suicide?

Of course it wasn't. You've simply pared down your professional contact database to those members with the potential to assist you in your ascent to the top. Now it's time to build it back up with new entries—value-added entries that can offer real opportunities for career advancement.

DISCRIMINATORY NETWORKING

In George Orwell's *Animal Farm*, the utopian commandment, "All animals are equal," established at the beginning of the novel, is eventually replaced by "All animals are equal, but some are more equal than others," as the pigs increasingly influence life on the farm. It's an interesting analogy for your list of contacts, particularly during a job search. It may be helpful to know everyone, but it really pays to know the special ones who will, hopefully, have an increasing impact on your career development. It's time for some "discriminatory networking."

Become more selective about whom you allow into the inner circle of your professional relationships. Continue to allow *everyone* into your overall network, just broaden your base. But focus your relationship-building energies on those who have the greatest potential to help you. As you rebuild your professional network, try to include:

- ☼ **Senior staff members of HR departments.** Many upper-management job openings are never advertised; even if they are, the first people to know about upcoming opportunities are the people who will have to fill the vacancies.

- ☼ **Executive recruiters.** Recruiters are frequently under contract with specific companies, so you want a number of carefully selected recruiters to know who you are. You may end up working closely with only one or two, but don't limit the number of recruiters who can connect you with your next job. As we mentioned in chapter 3, in the unlikely event that two recruiters are working for the same client, it's generally their responsibility to sort things out. However, if you know that each may be approaching the same company on your behalf, you should alert both recruiters to the potential conflict and monitor the situation.

- ☼ **"Connected" individuals in your industry.** The best places to hunt these people down are trade shows, conferences, conventions . . . any event that attracts a large number of professionals who work in your field. Who are they? They're the folks giving the keynote addresses, taking part in panel discussions, and leading the breakout sessions. Don't be shy; make it a point to establish relationships with them.

- ☼ **Ambitious individuals clearly on the way up the corporate ladder.** There's nothing wrong with using the "coattail" effect to enhance your career. You can identify the up-and-comers just by keeping your eyes and ears open. Build a rapport with them. If, as predicted, they rise toward the top, there's a very good chance they'll be taking people with them.

- ☼ **Mentors.** You will occasionally meet people who play virtually no role in the hiring process, have few true industry connections, are content with their current positions—and are *really* good at what they do. It would be a mistake to scratch these people from your professional network. While they probably won't directly help you find your way to that corner office, they can coach you into becoming a much more marketable commodity by improving your on-the-job performance. In addition, they may introduce you to others who can guide you upward.

Knowing whom *not* to include in your professional network is as important as knowing who *does* belong. As you cull through your current contacts (and make new ones), minimize the following:

- ☼ **Disgruntled employees.** They will be mood-killers at best, career-killers at worst. If it's obvious to you that someone is an unhappy (and probably unproductive) worker, you can be sure that it is just as obvious to upper management—and everyone is judged by the company they keep.

- ☼ **Users.** Networking is multidirectional. In order to harvest its fullest potential, the first networking benefit should flow *from* you *toward* someone else—a process we'll discuss later in this chapter. Be discerning; recognize that there are people out there who view networking purely on a "What can I get?" basis. They can't, and won't, help you. Don't help them. Decision makers value integrity. Don't associate yourself with people who have none.

- ☼ **Stagnant workers.** Don't confuse a mentor with a stagnant worker. A mentor may be truly content with his or her station in life; a stagnant worker simply accepts it. A mentor will want to help you achieve your goals and will provide expertise that can improve your performance; a stagnant worker has limited goals and won't be all that interested in helping you reach yours. This isn't to say that they're unpleasant people; they just don't bring much to the table as far as your career is concerned.

☼ **Employees with damaged reputations.** The quickest way to damage your good reputation is to be linked to someone with a bad reputation. Character counts, and it's likely that you have spent a considerable amount of time building yours in order to reach this point in your career. Reputations can be damaged in almost limitless ways—irresponsibility, insubordination, addiction, deception, unreliability, and dishonesty, to name just a few. Protect your reputation as you build your professional network; while there are many ways to damage a reputation, there are precious few ways to rebuild one.

A note: You may recognize some of your friends in the descriptions just listed. That's okay. We're not suggesting that you end your friendships, although you may want to make some of them a bit more discreet.

TURNING CONTACTS INTO RELATIONSHIPS

If you've followed our advice so far, your professional network now includes an awful lot of people you barely know—and it's difficult to imagine how people unfamiliar with you and your abilities can help you get ahead. Your task: Make them *want* to help you.

Act First

Don't expect a new contact to make the first move in your budding relationship. Be proactive, and offer something of value to her. Have access to courtside seats? Take one of your networking pals along with you. Not only will you be planting a huge "I owe you" seed in her soul, you'll have two or three hours of invaluable one-on-one time. (If the idea of spending this much time with a relative stranger causes you to develop nervous tics, give both tickets to your new contact. She'll enjoy the game and likely still be inclined to reciprocate in some way. You'll lose the one-on-one time, but you'll have taken a significant step toward the contact-to-relationship conversion.)

Never Ask for a Job

Neediness is never pretty. It may be crucial for you to find a job as soon as possible, but if you come across as desperate, you'll burn bridges before they're even built. Seek advice, not employment. People who barely know you will usually be happy to offer advice, but rarely will they come through with a job offer.

Know Their Interests

You want them to get to know you, right? Know them first. During conversations, pick up clues as to hobbies, outside interests, family life—anything that helps you move beyond connecting a name to a job title and little else. A small act—something as innocuous as forwarding along a magazine article of interest with a note asking, "Did you see this?"—can pay big dividends in the long run. It's another proactive move designed to foster the "payback" mentality. Plus, everyone appreciates seemingly random acts of thoughtfulness.

Labor Over Your Resume

You should know this by now, but in case you don't: Stop sending out generic copies of your resume. Doing so reveals an entry-level job-seeking mentality on your part. If you're asked to provide a resume—by anyone—craft it specifically for that particular person at that particular company, who (hopefully) has told you about a particular opening. New members of your professional network won't ask for your resume for no reason at all; they probably know of something that may be a good fit for you. Don't embarrass them by forwarding a cookie-cutter resume. (For more resume tips, see chapter 6.)

Be Consistently Gracious

Get in the habit of sending thank-you cards for every favor, however small. Everyone likes to feel appreciated. In the same vein, avoid using e-mail as a substitute for real mail during the holiday season. Take the time to "snail-mail" holiday greetings to every professional member of your network. Yes, it's a time-killer. Yes, it could mean hundreds of dollars in postage fees. And yes…it does make a difference.

JOIN THE CLUB

As you compile your network, recognize that many networks of great benefit to you already exist:

- ☿ If you're a business school graduate, join the alumni association. The Wharton School of Business, for example, has almost eighty thousand alumni. For that matter, joining the alumni association of any university you attended is a worthwhile endeavor.

- ☿ Seek out local networks that cater exclusively to high-earning individuals in your region; they exist in all major U.S. metropolitan areas. Sometimes,

From the Desk of

Keith Ferrazzi
CEO, Ferrazzi Greenlight

Whenever people are looking for their next high-level jobs, inevitably someone chimes in with something to the effect of, "What kind of work/life balance will that position afford you?" I'm sick and tired of hearing questions like that, all too often in the tone of a nit-picking mother-in-law, about the "atrocity" that is today's out-of-balance executive.

I'm here to say that we are only out of balance if we say we are. We shouldn't let anybody else tell us what balance is. Only we can define it. The widespread idea of balance as some sort of an equation, from which we could take this many hours from one side of our lives and give it to another side and suddenly be happy, is a total myth. Balance is too personal to be an equation.

You'll do better to focus not on balancing, but *blending*. Overlapping the personal, professional, and community components of your life will help you build stronger relationships for your success and get more done in less time. For example, I love bringing clients into my home for dinner parties. Since business relationships are personal relationships, there's no better way to become endeared to my clients than by sharing hearth and home. It also allows me to share the time with those I love. My friends and family can actually enjoy the interaction with new, interesting people, and not be shut out of my life because I've gone to yet another strictly business dinner.

When you find your next executive position, don't worry about how you'll separate your work from your life. Instead, ask how you can use it to blur the boundaries in your life to simultaneously enhance your joy and achievement in personal, professional, and community endeavors.

Keith Ferrazzi is the author of New York Times *best-seller* Never Eat Alone *(www.NeverEatAlone.com).*

these geography-specific organizations have a narrow focus, such as the New York Commercial Real Estate Women Network (www.nycrew.org). Look around; you may be able to dramatically increase your list of contacts by joining a single well-connected group.

☼ Industry-specific networks can be a gold mine for job leads, assuming that most members are already employed. The National Banking and Financial Services Network (www.nbn-jobs.com) is one example of this type of network. However, if you work in an industry (or in a geographic region) with significant unemployment, joining one of these groups will feel less like a networking opportunity and more like a "misery loves company" club.

☼ Demand exclusivity. Earlier in this chapter we talked about the hierarchy pyramid that exists in almost all companies. Very few people have access to the top. For that reason, you want to make sure the executive networks you join have barriers to entry—otherwise, they're not really "executive" networks. Obstacles to entry can come in the form of salary requirements (many start in the $75,000 to $100,000 range), membership limits (one member per industry), or other criteria. The DuPage Executive Network (www.cod.edu/secure/den), for example, qualifies its membership by geographic region (metropolitan Chicago), minimum salary (at least $75,000), and/or job title.

THE PEOPLE YOU NEVER MEET

Effective networking isn't always about face-to-face encounters; thanks to technology, you can get a lot of mileage from contacts with people you've never met. Online networking (as well as the burgeoning blog trend, which we discussed earlier) can connect you with others in your field, providing a possible link to your next job.

Online networks provide the ability to quickly and efficiently share information; they can be industry-specific or more general. LinkedIn, for example, is an online network of more than three million professionals across the world. Jobster, an invitation-only networking site, connects professionals and employers through referrals. And even primarily social sites like Friendster can offer valuable networking opportunities.

As you begin to seek out and communicate with new members of your network, make sure to take advantage of this valuable networking tool.

take a memo

Stay Active Online

Be advised: You should be just as active (probably more so) in "faceless" online groups as you are in your community networks, because online groups tend to have a heightened awareness of member inactivity. You're already "out of sight"; you can't afford to be "out of mind."

NEVER NEGLECT NETWORKING AGAIN

After reading this chapter, don't be surprised if you view networking differently. You should! It would be a mistake to treat your professional network too casually. Everyone you meet has the potential to join this network; it's your job to determine if they should. If you're hoping to swell the ranks of your contact list, consider a couple of targeted professional memberships.

Networking offers one of the fastest paths to the corner office you covet. True, you could stumble across an ideal opportunity all on your own. But you'll boost your odds greatly by bolstering your network.

RECOMMENDED BOOKS

Dig Your Well Before You're Thirsty: The Only Networking Book You'll Ever Need by Harvey Mackay (Doubleday, 1999, ISBN 0385485468, $15.95).

The Executive Job Search: A Comprehensive Handbook for Seasoned Professionals by Orrin G. Wood (McGraw-Hill, 2003, ISBN 0071409424, $15.95).

A Foot in the Door: Networking Your Way into the Hidden Job Market by Katharine Hansen (Ten Speed Press, 2000, ISBN 1580081401, $14.95).

Make Your Contacts Count: Networking Know-How for Cash, Clients, and Career Success by Anne Baber and Lynn Waymon (AMACOM, 2001, ISBN 0814470939, $14.95).

Networking with the Affluent by Thomas J. Stanley (McGraw-Hill, 1997, ISBN 0070610487, $17.95).

Never Eat Alone: And Other Secrets to Success, One Relationship at a Time by Keith Ferrazzi (Currency, 2005, ISBN 0385512058, $24.95).

Nonstop Networking: How to Improve Your Life, Luck, and Career by Andrea R. Nierenberg (Capital Books, 2002, ISBN 1892123924, $19.95).

RECOMMENDED WEB SITES

Netshare—Membership-based networking organization for high-income professionals:
http://www.netshare.com

ecademy—Online networking portal:
http://www.ecademy.com

LinkedIn—Joins together people, jobs, and services:
http://www.linkedin.com

Jobster—Invitation-only network connecting employers with recommended professionals:
http://www.jobster.com

Friendster—Reach more than 20 million members online:
http://www.friendster.com

Seven Ways to Maximize the Value of Networking Meetings:
http://www.executiveagent.com/career/archives/20030729_main.html

Networking Strategies for Shy Professionals:
http://www.careerjournal.com/jobhunting/networking

Online Networking Tips:
http://www.entrepreneur.com/article/0,4621,322995,00.html

CHAPTER 6

Survival of the Fittest: Your Resume Evolves

"This résumé appears to cover only the last forty-five minutes."

Remember the dot-com bust a few years back? More than fifty thousand workers lost their jobs in a sixteen-month period beginning in late 1999. Hundreds of companies closed up shop, many with virtually no notice to their customers or employees. Personal fortunes were lost—or, more accurately, never realized in the first place. Over time, the free fall spilled over into other industries, pulling the United States into a recession.

However, something good *did* come out of all the chaos: American workers began to pay more attention to their resumes. Even today, surveys show that almost 40 percent of workers have up-to-date resumes, and an equal number believe theirs are somewhat ready for distribution with very little notice.

Even if you updated your resume just last week, this chapter is worth reading. Here you'll discover how to tailor your resume to each individual who receives it. We'll also reveal how to strengthen the contents of your resume, the most common mistakes to avoid, and other information that could place your resume at the top of the stack.

KEEPING IT FRESH

Imagine that you've held the same job for the past four years. Your supervisor hasn't changed, and neither have your responsibilities. You haven't updated your resume all this time because it is still a valid, up-to-date resume—at least in your view.

It's possible that your resume is in satisfactory shape. It's also probable that it doesn't provide an accurate glimpse into your current abilities. If this scenario sounds familiar, it's time to take steps to guard against resume complacency.

Your life includes two documents that should be revised on a regular basis. The first, your will, distributes your wealth after you die; the second, your resume, helps you amass that wealth in the first place. Life's ever-changing nature (births, deaths, marriages, divorces, and so on) is incentive enough for most people to amend their wills periodically. Similarly, you need to take a fresh look at your resume as your career evolves—even if your employer and job title have remained unchanged for some time.

Why? Because *you're* evolving. It's possible to stay in the same job for years while continuing to strengthen your skills and marketability as a future leader. Your resume must reflect this.

Updating your resume also provides an opportunity for you to "inventory" your assets. A resume plays up your strong points, but it can reveal your weaknesses as well. Leadership demands a mix of both hard and soft skills, with an increasing emphasis on the latter. As you cast a critical eye over your resume, see whether it leans too heavily toward hard skills while failing to highlight your soft skills, such as team-building or the ability to motivate reluctant employees. (For a further look at hard and soft skills, see "Focusing on Soft Skills" later in this chapter.)

IF THE POSITION FITS, TAILOR IT

Think way back to your final days in college, when you spent hours perfecting your resume, agonizing over every comma, verb tense, bullet, and word choice. You read and reread your resume repeatedly, tweaked it endlessly, labored over which paper stock to use—and then ordered dozens, if not hundreds, of copies from a local printer to carpet-bomb every employer within a fifty-mile radius.

Although you found a job, you did so very inefficiently. It didn't much matter then, because you were only seeking an entry-level position. Even today, this mass-blanketing method is how most college graduates land their first jobs.

You, however, are hoping to achieve a position in upper management. Remember the corporate hierarchy pyramid: The pool of leadership jobs in each company is much smaller than the pool of jobs further down the food chain. Accordingly, you need to be selective about which ones you pursue—and you need to craft a different resume for each one.

Today, it is possible for you to create and print at home one-of-a-kind, targeted resumes, *so each resume you send out should be unique*. It should be tailored for the individual or company receiving it. A "generic" resume creates the perception that you're not interested in a specific company or position, and it will kill your chance at winning an initial interview. These cookie-cutter resumes present you as a job seeker casting a wide and indiscriminate net in the search for your next position.

Customizing your resume can be as involved as shifting, or eliminating, entire sections: Work history may be important to one prospective employer, while another may be more interested in your skills and performance. If you have the opportunity to receive input from someone with inside knowledge about the job you're interested in, ask for specifics. It will help you determine the proper approach your resume should take.

COVER ME!

While we would never think of downplaying the resume's significance (which is why this entire chapter is devoted to the subject), the reality is that your resume is not the most important document you'll send a potential employer. That honor belongs to your cover letter. And, surprisingly, most people spend far less time on the cover letter than on the resume.

hot facts

By the Letter

A survey by the Society for Human Resource Management shows that recruiters will probably spend less than three minutes looking at your resume. Most start with your cover letter and determine after reading it whether or not your resume is worth a glance.

Your resume is a somewhat dry recitation of the facts surrounding your career to date. Your cover letter, on the other hand, can have pizzazz. It can exude personality, confidence, and other qualities that the recipient is hoping to stumble across as she wades through a pile of job candidates' submissions. It can demonstrate your ability to communicate effectively, a critical trait for those in leadership positions.

Alternatively, a poorly written cover letter makes the reader doubt your talents, question your potential, and view your ability to communicate with skepticism—effectively ending your shot at an interview.

But what constitutes a good cover letter—or a bad one, for that matter? Examine the following characteristics of ineffective and effective cover letters:

Ineffective Cover Letter	**Effective Cover Letter**
Language is weak and uninteresting; some words, particularly verbs, are overused to the point of redundancy. A good rule of thumb is to limit your use of each verb to only once per letter. Instead of writing *supervised* 3–4 times in your cover letter, try *led, implemented, created, directed . . .* you get the picture.	Displays a strong ability to communicate through the use of "vivid verbs" and other language that engages the mind of the reader. Vivid verbs are written in active voice and are much more descriptive than their overused counterparts. For example, did you know that there are at least 200 different verbs you can substitute for the verb *said*?

Ineffective Cover Letter	Effective Cover Letter
Repeats information found on the resume, often word for word. Remember: The resume is a litany of your career so far. It's a look at your past; your cover letter should focus on the future.	Serves as an introduction, an expression of your desire for a specific position, and an explanation of your goals once you're in that position. Unlike your resume, it's a forward-looking document. It's fine to elaborate on your past accomplishments, but only to provide details not covered in the resume.
Shows telltale signs of being generic. *Never* address it "To Whom It May Concern"; likewise, avoid talking about your career goals in general terms. You are seeking a specific leadership position. Address it head-on.	Comes across as being very carefully researched because it is addressed to a specific person, explicitly states the job being sought, and mentions details about the company that demonstrate your interest in joining it.
Raises red flags by focusing on salary requirements while at the same time not outlining why you want a "change of scenery" in the first place.	Spells out the reasons for seeking the job in question. Does not mention salary (that's a discussion best reserved for a later time). The only exception to this is in cases where you are sending your cover letter, along with your resume, to an executive recruiter. Recruiters need this information in order to assess your candidacy.
The concluding paragraph does not restate the position in which you are interested, does not thank the recipient for taking the time to read the letter, ends abruptly, and gives the reader a "left hanging" feeling.	Generally takes up only one page and is visually appealing (for example, no awkward-looking margins, size-eight font, or overuse of boldface type and/or italics). Includes a well-written final paragraph that is gracious and at the same time recaps the central points contained in the letter.

A couple of final thoughts: Typographical and grammatical errors will sound the death knell for any job candidacy. And while bullets are appropriate on your resume, allowing you to succinctly summarize your qualifications, avoid using bullets in your cover letter. A cover letter is your chance to highlight your verbal ability, so use a smooth narrative style that reflects your personality, enthusiasm, and fit for the position.

You cannot review your cover letter (or your resume) enough. We advocate drafting your own resumes and cover letters; you will achieve a familiarity with your work history that could serve you well during an interview (we'll discuss this further in chapter 7). However, consider hiring a professional firm to help craft your resume and cover letter if you are unsure of your abilities in this area.

DISSECTING THE RESUME

Many people consider themselves to be competent resume writers. It's an understandable assumption, particularly for those who have rewritten their resumes several times over. Landing a job is proof enough that your resume-creation skills are up to snuff, right?

Well, yes and no. As we mentioned above, creating and updating your resume reinforces your familiarity with your experience and skill set. However, that same familiarity can blind you to weaknesses in the document. All writers eventually fall in love with their own words, which is why editors exist.

take a memo

The "Magic Bullet" Theory

No one likes to read endless pages of text, and that's especially true for people who cull through resumes for a living. Break down your resume entries into bulleted items—it will create a much more visually appealing document, and it will help focus the reader on specific statements.

However, don't overdo it! Limit your use of bullets for each position you've held to four or five maximum. Each bulleted entry should be as brief as possible (otherwise, you're simply creating bulleted paragraphs). Try to keep each bulleted item on one or two lines; you can explain the details more fully either in your cover letter or (hopefully) in an interview.

Guard against this by having your friends, peers, family members, or a professional resume-writing service look over your resume before you submit it. Also, consider the following suggestions. Some may seem a bit remedial, but you might discover a couple of ways to enhance your resume.

Job Objective

Although you may have heard this referred to as the most important line on your resume, the reality is that, at your level, it's usually inappropriate to include an objective on your resume. The "job objective" is important when you're mass-mailing generic resumes to several employers. You, however, will be targeting each resume to a specific audience and crafting unique cover letters for each one. For that reason, eliminate the objective altogether. You now have one less thing to worry about, and you've freed up a little bit of real estate on your resume that you can use more effectively.

Work History

You can approach this section in one of two ways, each of which has its own merits. The most common approach is to go in reverse chronological order (most recent position first), because doing so will highlight your latest accomplishments. This is the method that we recommend. (For an example of this type of resume, see page 88.)

If you've switched careers, or have moved from job to job with somewhat diverse responsibilities each time you've changed employers, using the reverse-chronological method can get a bit confusing. In that case, try the second approach: Group your employment data according to the skills and accomplishments you've acquired. Although the dates may be a bit difficult to follow, the person reading the resume will have a much easier time identifying your strengths and achievements as they relate to the job opening. However, be sure not to leave large, obvious gaps in your work history. These may raise a red flag to the employer or recruiter.

Other Skills

Few people work in a vacuum. You may have spent the past ten years in accounting while becoming adept at contract negotiation. Or you could have had primary responsibility for staff development and, out of necessity, learned the intricacies of handling a large budget. The point is this: You probably have developed skills that fall outside the normal parameters of your various job titles. If so, there may be no easy way to draw attention to them in the "Work History" category of your resume. That's what the "Other Skills" section is designed to address.

For example, while working as a human resources benefits representative in a large company, David—a self-described "computer buff"—streamlined an online database so his boss could maintain employee records more efficiently. His work got the attention of a manager in charge of fulfilling customer orders, who asked David if he could create a program that would keep track of customer preferences and automatically send a reminder to salespeople to approach customers when it was time to place new orders. David developed a program that worked so well that it was distributed to other regional offices.

Clearly, this would be a difficult, and awkward, fit under the heading of "HR representative" on David's resume. By placing it in the "Other Skills" section, David was better able to highlight this accomplishment and present himself as an employee with a broader skills base. Here's how he noted it:

OTHER SKILLS
During off-work hours, I created a proprietary program to track client inventory and alert our sales personnel of potential incoming purchase orders. This proved so effective that it was adopted by all our regional offices.

Don't worry if you find that you cannot quantify your "Other Skills" into a neat section on your resume. This section is optional (note that it's not included in the sample resume on page 88). You may feel that accomplishments not clearly related to your job title are best saved for the interview. This can be a springboard into a conversation that falls outside the scope of your resume and may open the door for you to ask questions of your own.

Additional Information

Unless you've been in the workforce for at least twenty years, you probably don't need this section. You're better off finding a way to fold this information into the "Work History" area of your resume. In the event that you *have* been working for twenty to thirty years, it's probably a good idea to condense the first few years into this section (although you may want to consider removing this information from your resume entirely, as long as it doesn't raise questions about gaps in employment). Because it follows your "Work History" keep the information contained here to a minimum—rarely will your accomplishments twenty-five years ago be of any value in finding a job now. If you believe very strongly that one of these jobs provided you with skills that are still useful today, stress it in the "Other Skills" section.

Betty, a forty-nine-year-old CFO candidate, began her career in media relations. After completing her MBA degree twenty years ago, she moved away from staff jobs and into line positions. Although she doesn't want to include low-level (and irrelevant) job titles in the "Employment History" section of her resume, she does want to stress her skills as a communicator. This section is tailor-made for that task. Betty addressed it in this manner:

ADDITIONAL INFORMATION
I believe communication is a valuable tool for executives. I began my career in media relations, and I am comfortable dealing with media requests, internal communications, and external announcements.

Note that in the sample resume on page 88, the job hunter summarizes her major accomplishments, including media appearances, published work, and speaking engagements, in the "Additional Information" section. If you have leadership roles in professional organizations or media experience related to your industry, be sure to highlight these achievements on your resume.

RESUME KILLERS

Hiring managers and recruiters analyze resumes for a living; they're conditioned to sniff out "red flags" that can end your candidacy for a position before it even begins. Put yourself in their shoes as you review your resume. Despite your best efforts, you'll probably find some of the following problems that need addressing.

Achievements Are Not Clearly Defined
Many people make the mistake of spelling out their responsibilities instead of outlining their accomplishments. Your resume shouldn't read like a job description. It should emphasize your successes, because your successes are what will help you land an interview.

Take a look at the two samples below. One highlights the candidate's current duties, while the other focuses on results. Which would grab your attention if you were in charge of finding a national advertising sales director for a Fortune 500 company?

During the past three years, I have had primary responsibility for our East Coast sales network.

Or:

During my tenure as East Coast sales director, our revenues have increased nearly 75 percent.

Dates Are Missing or Minimized

There are three major reasons why people leave dates of employment off their resumes:

1. To hide long gaps in employment (see below).

2. To minimize the appearance of "job-hopping" when several positions have been held in a short period of time.

3. To ward off possible age discrimination.

Missing dates raise eyebrows. As tempting as it may be to remove dates from your resume, you'll do more damage to your job search than good by omitting them. True, you may have some explaining to do, particularly for reasons 1 and 2. But a well-written cover letter can go a long way toward addressing those issues, and you can explain yourself more fully during the interview.

Gaps in Employment

These are not quite as deadly as they once were; the staggering number of job losses just a few years ago legitimizes most employment interruptions, *as long as the reasons are valid*. Besides a mass layoff, other justifiable reasons for a gap in employment include:

- ☼ **A lengthy illness.** However, you're on treacherous ground here, because you don't want prospective employers to view you as sickly or a health risk. You can address the circumstances briefly in a cover letter, or explain (as fully as you comfortably feel you can) the specifics of the situation during the interview.

- ☼ **Family matters,** such as taking care of an elderly parent.

- ☼ **A much-needed (and deserved) sabbatical.** Say, for instance, you played your cards just right during the dot-com boom and cashed in ahead of the dot-com bust, amassing a sizable amount of wealth. (Not every worker lost his or her shirt in the fallout.) You may have taken a fifteen-month tour of Europe and Asia; it's difficult to account for this on a resume.

In these cases, one gap is probably acceptable. More than that? Be prepared for close scrutiny.

Miscellaneous Information Detracts from Your Presentation

Never include a section with personal information such as hobbies and community or social involvement. These things have nothing to do with the task at hand, and you can find more effective uses for the space. Likewise, do not send a picture along with your resume as an attempt to highlight your "youthful" appearance if you are seeking to fit into a particular corporate culture.

Finally, remove the "References Available Upon Request" line. It's unnecessary, since you will be asked to provide multiple references if you become a candidate of interest.

Trying to Fit It All on One Page

Years ago, conventional wisdom held that resumes had to be kept to one page. However, workers now change employers with more frequency than in the past, and this recommendation is no longer an ironclad rule. Given that you are vying for an upper-management post, it's expected that your resume will be longer than one page. It's better to use a second page rather than downsize the font in an effort to follow this outdated standard. At the same time, avoid using a third page. Unless you've already held several leadership posts or are an academic, a three-page resume will come across as verbose. Be concise; this reinforces your reputation as a skilled communicator, and it makes the resume much easier to digest.

"Laundry-listing" Your Entire Career

Your work history should go back only ten to fifteen years. If you insist on including titles and job descriptions from long ago, create an "Additional Experience" section, as explained above—and be succinct.

Embellishments

We discussed the marks of leadership back in chapter 1, and integrity was at the top of the list. Misleading statements on your resume will end your candidacy. Worse, they can actually cost you the job after you've been hired.

Academic records and achievements are frequently exaggerated on resumes, although they're the easiest for recruiters and hiring managers to verify. A misleading resume will portray you as someone with a disturbing lack of character, and successful leaders do not suffer from a lack of character.

Want proof of the consequences of "stretching the truth" on your resume? How would you like to be the subject of the following wire stories?

December 14, 2001

O'LEARY OUT AT NOTRE DAME AFTER ONE WEEK

SOUTH BEND, Ind. (AP)—George O'Leary resigned as Notre Dame football coach five days after being hired, admitting he lied about his academic and athletic background.

O'Leary claimed to have a master's degree in education and to have played college football for three years, but checks into his background showed it wasn't true.

October 16, 2003

DUCHANE ADMITS LYING ON RESUME

STERLING HEIGHTS—City Manager Steve Duchane acknowledged that he lied about his college credentials, but said he would not quit his $123,000-per-year job as chief executive of Metro Detroit's second-largest suburb.

Duchane said in an interview with *The Detroit News* that he also used deceit about his academic record earlier in his career to get hired by other cities.

He told *The News* he attended classes at Washtenaw Community College but never earned a degree there and that he never attended Franklin University in Columbus, Ohio. Documents in personnel files obtained by *The News* showed Duchane claimed to have degrees from those schools to get city management jobs in Howell and Corunna, near Flint.

"I had some good-intentioned help from some people," Duchane said. "This is a small screwup that's gotten bigger and bigger. But look at it now. I've ruined my life."

—Tony Manolatos, *Detroit News*

Resume or Curriculum Vitae (CV)?

Many American workers are unfamiliar with the *curriculum vitae*, and for good reason: It is infrequently used unless you work in academia. However, if you are seeking a job overseas, you should expect to be asked to provide a CV.

CVs are similar to resumes, but have a much heavier emphasis on academic achievements, organizational memberships, and publishing successes. They also run longer (three pages or more) than a conventional resume. Be fore-warned: Many CV recipients expect details that would never be found on an "American" resume, such as age, hobbies, and nationality.

Focusing on Soft Skills

You're probably already familiar with hard and soft skills, so consider this a possibly much-needed refresher. Hard skills involve a mastery of concrete tasks: the ability to use technology, for example, or your talent for itemizing a budget. These skills likely have proven valuable in getting you to this point in your career. They will continue to be important as you move forward, and you should welcome any opportunity to bolster them or add to your repertoire.

However, it's the soft skills that most accurately predict your future success as a leader. You may be a numbers whiz in the accounting department, but if you have a difficult time with team-building or motivating other employees, you're probably not going to be a very effective chief financial officer. You can be a tremendously polished public speaker (an example of a hard skill), but if you can't effectively communicate with those around you—and get them to buy into your vision—you won't be a productive leader.

Here's a sampling of some soft skills you should be acquiring as you inch your way toward the corner office:

☼ **Quiet confidence.** This has a double meaning. You should project an air of calm, collected self-assurance regardless of how dire a situation may get. If you do, you will instill a quiet confidence in the people around you that things are not as bad as they seem—as long as you're in charge.

☼ **Team-building and consensus-building.** It's so much easier to lead when those being led want to follow. Avoid the "my way or the highway" stance; instead, strive to convert the nonbelievers to your way of think-ing. If you get them to buy into your plan, you've paved a smooth path toward your objective.

☼ **Communication.** Every person on your team needs to feel as if he or she is "in the loop" at all times. Make it a point to let those around you know exactly what's happening, *as soon* as it's happening. Uncertainty breeds fear, and fear breeds paranoia. Paranoia, in turn, breeds paralysis and divisiveness.

☼ **Attention to detail.** This is not the same thing as micromanaging. Very few staff members appreciate being micromanaged, because it makes them feel as if they aren't trusted to do their jobs or to make responsible decisions. Know what those around you are doing, but trust them to do it right and hold them accountable for producing results.

☼ **Diplomacy.** You are free to dislike anyone and despise every aspect of the workplace around you. However, keep it to yourself if you want to get ahead. Once spoken, your words can never be taken back—and there are probably plenty of people all too willing to publicize your words (and actions) if it will cast you in a bad light while simultaneously improving how they are perceived. Act presidential. Those in a position to aid your ascension will notice it.

☼ **Creative problem solving.** Otherwise known as "thinking outside the box." Times change, and so, too, do solutions. Cultivate the capacity to find innovative ways out of challenging situations.

☼ **Motivational ability.** You can't fake this on a long-term basis; without results, even your most gung-ho attitude will soon fall on deaf ears. The best way to increase your knack for motivating people is to develop the other soft skills previously listed. Most staff members will be motivated to follow a leader they believe in.

A WORD ABOUT REFERENCES

As we've discussed, you want to eliminate references on your resume. They're unnecessary and take up valuable resume real estate. You are not going to win an upper-management job without having your references carefully vetted. For that matter, be prepared (as we discussed back in chapter 2) to have your credit history and personal background thoroughly investigated as well.

The good news: If you've been asked to provide references, you can assume you're a serious candidate for the position. The not-so-good news: If you have skeletons in your closet, you'd be wise to explain them in advance.

A forthcoming and earnest appearance is essential for leadership. The level of scrutiny into your past will often depend on the level of the position you're seeking, and a diligent investigation could reveal things you never thought would see the light of day again. Be proactive instead of reactive, and you'll never have to worry about long-ago deeds or circumstances coming out at a most inopportune time.

Now, about those references—whom should you use?

▶ **Action Items: Who Will Vouch for You?**
Before reading further, jot down the five references you would provide if you were asked to do so at this very moment.

1. _____

2. _____

3. _____

4. _____

5. _____

Now let's look at what effective references are and see how you've done.

> ☼ The first rule of thumb with references is that each one should be a professional, not a personal, reference. If someone on your list cannot vouch for your abilities in the workplace, their input will be rejected. Personal references are acceptable for entry-level positions only.

> ☼ Before listing the human resources department (or your boss) at your current place of employment, ask if they will provide an honest and candid appraisal of your accomplishments. Many companies—particularly those among the Fortune 500—will simply furnish dates of employment out of a fear of possible litigation. This type of reference will undermine your superb performance, because it invites second-guessing on the part of the interviewer about why your reference is reticent to discuss your work.

> ☼ Are your references aware of every aspect of your job search? It's not enough that they know you're looking. Your references need to know the details: the company you've contacted, the job title you're pursuing, and the responsibilities of the position. This allows them to tailor their responses accordingly. Before you send the resume, spend some time prepping the references you'll be providing if you receive a call.

☼ You customize your resume for each position you seek; you should do the same with your references. Develop a network of ten to twelve possible references. Identify the strengths each can provide to your job search. As you send your resumes out, make a note about which references you'd like to use for each position. Again, let them know in advance that they should expect a possible phone call regarding your candidacy.

☼ Using subordinates as references is acceptable. Who best to explain your rapport with your staff? Make sure you use only those staffers who can speak eloquently, and with ease, about your abilities. *Never* demand that one of your subordinates (or anyone, actually) act as a reference. Your references must be willing to sell you of their own volition; when they are, their enthusiasm for your abilities will become apparent to the interviewer.

A WORD ABOUT E-MAILING RESUMES

Many employers accept resumes via e-mail for posted positions, so you need to get over any apprehensions you may have about submitting yours in this manner. However, there are a few unofficial items of protocol to keep in mind:

Check first before sending. Not every company embraces this submission method, particularly smaller firms that may have been burned previously by computer viruses piggybacking their way into the office.

When seeking approval from the hiring manager to forward your resume by e-mail, verify the preferred format (i.e., Word document attachment or plain-text e-mail). Also give her *your* originating e-mail address. This will help separate your message from any unsolicited e-mails that may clutter the same inbox. As a final gesture of goodwill, call to alert her that it has been sent.

Don't be contagious. The fastest way to end your candidacy is to transfer an infected file within your e-mail. Keep your antivirus programs up-to-date, and scan your resume at least twice before attaching it to an e-mail. Many e-mail programs will scan your outgoing messages as well, providing further assurances that your message is virus-free.

Send it to yourself first. The natural tendency is to get your resume in as quickly as possible. Resist this urge to forge ahead. When you believe your resume is ready for transmission, e-mail it to yourself (along with the cover letter that will form the body of the message to which your resume may be attached). When it arrives, open the e-mail. Read it slowly and carefully, and then open the attached file. If you encounter problems opening the attachment, it's a near-certainty that the hiring manager will as well. For maximum peace of mind, open the e-mail with a different computer than you used to send it, in order to get a truer sense of how everything will work on the other end.

Offer a contingency plan. Even within companies that allow electronic resume submission, there will be people who are squeamish about opening e-mail attachments. For that reason, it's a good idea to provide a link to your online resume, if you have one. If you do this, make sure that you're not directing the hiring manager to a generic resume; post the exact resume you want him to see and give him a specific URL to visit. This is most easily done if you've previously set up a personal Web site or maintain a blog. Cast a critical eye on your posted resume. Remove hit counters and eliminate any links that appear to be wayward or could distract your visitor/potential employer. (If you're considering creating a personal Web site, sites such as http://smallbusiness.yahoo.com or http://360.yahoo.com offer free and low-cost Web hosting packages; you may also want to consult a professional Web designer to ensure your site is clear and easy to navigate.)

Seek help if needed. If you're not comfortable dealing with e-mail or e-mail attachments, enlist the aid of someone who is. Venturing into uncharted territory could cause you to commit a variety of mistakes (multiple inadvertent messages, wrong recipients) that will hurt your candidacy.

take a memo

Online Applications

If you are applying for a position online through a company's Web site (or are directed to a company's online application page from a job board like Yahoo! HotJobs), you may be instructed to cut and paste your resume directly into an online form. Be aware that much of your formatting may be lost. Consider first creating a plain-text version of your resume using tools like Notepad or Wordpad. Keep the organization clean and simple: Use all-caps instead of boldface, asterisks instead of bullet points, etc.

Sara L. Hanson

123 Main Street, Anytown, NY 12345

Home: (555) 555-8583   Cell: (555) 555-4282   E-Mail: sara_l_hanson@yahoo.com

Marketing Executive: 15 years experience creating marketing campaigns for multi-national, midsize, and start-up graphics software companies. Reputation as an innovative marketer with expertise in translating consumer insights into winning value propositions and compelling messaging. Build leading brands, apply strong analytical/strategic thinking to grow revenue and profit, and lead marketing organizations at a significant scale.

Experience

GREAT GRAPHICS, INC., New York, NY   1998–Present

Direct 25 employees in developing and implementing effective marketing plans. Manage consumer research, go-to-market strategies and execution, branding and packaging, direct mail, affiliate and search marketing, channel programs, training, and operations.

Vice President, Corporate Marketing   2001–Present

- Reorganized marketing function to better align with business priorities; upgraded talent and methodologies; improved utilization of funding and vendors; and enhanced research design, planning, and reporting capabilities.
- Delivered incremental revenue of over $25M in 2005 by improving effectiveness of Web, phone, and direct mail campaigns.
- Direct retail presence via packaging and Web strategies. Increased product trial and customer acquisition while reducing development time by 50%, saving $2.5M.
- Create brand architecture, positioning, and messaging, delivering a more coherent consumer brand experience.
- Enabled four new product launches by improving and streamlining critical marketing processes, creating sustainable growth for a $1B franchise.

Vice President and GM, Telco and Media   1998–2001

- Effectively navigated challenging team and strategic-partner dynamics to lead a multi-functional team in launching a brokerage service within a seven-month time frame.
- Restructured online advertising pricing matrix, delivering $16M in incremental revenue.
- Improved sales pipeline forecasting capabilities, generating incremental revenue of $15M.

GRAFFIX GROUP, LTD., San Francisco, CA   1993–1998

Managed brand awareness and equity, advertising, media planning, packaging, segmentation, targeting, research, volume forecasting, budgeting, business analysis, and pricing functions.

Recognitions and Awards: Outstanding Coaching, Envisioning Success, Strategic Thinking, Leveraging Diversity, and People's Choice Print Advertising.

Sara L. Hanson   Page two

Sr. Brand Manager, New Business Research & Development   1995–1998
- Designed and implemented consumer research studies for U.S., Japan, and Latin America.
- Created a new women's gaming brand in a primarily male market by redefining the product value proposition. Brand generated $250M in revenue in year one.
- Drove ongoing risk evaluation, delivering consumer market test six months ahead of schedule.

Brand Manager, Games Group   1994–1995
- Oversaw the development of TV, radio, print, and co-branded advertising for the Graffix Gaming brand.
- Overcame management skepticism of Graffix Gaming's ability to succeed in the Hispanic market by conducting a comprehensive analysis and developing the first-ever integrated ethnic marketing model, growing unit volume by 15% and gaining management's confidence to increase spending by 400%.
- Led annual business reviews, providing analysis and recommendations for maintaining core business while launching new initiatives.

Assistant Brand Manager, Education Group   1993–1994
- Led cross-functional team in determining the feasibility and strategic fit of a line extension through consumer research and competitive, pricing, and financial analysis.
- Developed promotion analysis models to evaluate marketing program effectiveness, saving $800K.

XYZ START-UP CORPORATION, Santa Clara, CA   1990–1993
Product Manager, Digital Media
- Founding member of start-up. Developed first 24-bit color and video for the Mac. IPO 1992.

Education
- MBA, Stanford University, Stanford, CA, 1995. *Dean's List*
- BA, Broadcast Journalism, Columbia University, New York, NY, 1988. *Cum Laude*

Additional Information
- Recognized expert in computer graphics for special effects and postproduction; appeared on *60 Minutes* to demonstrate how computers create special effects.
- Published work includes papers for *Graphics Quarterly*, *Computers & Video*, and numerous trade journals on the subjects of computer graphics and image processing.
- Keynote speaker on sharing of advanced technologies between government and entertainment sectors at Graphics World Expo 1998.

A WORK IN PERPETUAL PROGRESS

If you're feeling a bit less confident about the state of your resume by now, don't worry. Your resume will never be perfect, because it's an evolving document. Your job is to ensure that it's as good as it can be at the moment you submit it.

Don't wait until you're knee-deep in a job search to revise it; instead, revisit your resume annually when you're not in a job search and much more frequently when you're planning one. Anxiety now is much better than anxiety later, after you've shipped your resume off to a potential employer. By following the suggestions outlined in this chapter, we're confident that your resume will demonstrate your readiness to move into the corner office.

RECOMMENDED BOOKS

Asher's Bible of Executive Resumes and How to Write Them by Donald Asher (Ten Speed Press, 1996, ISBN 0898158567, $32.50).

Best Cover Letters for $100,000+ Jobs by Wendy S. Enelow (Impact Publications, 2001, ISBN 1570231699, $24.95).

CareerJournal.com Resume Guide for $100,000+ Executive Jobs by William E. Montag (Wiley, 2002, ISBN 0471232874, $21.95).

Contagious Success: Spreading High Performance Throughout Your Organization by Susan Lucia Annunzio (Portfolio, 2004, ISBN 1591840600, $24.95).

e-Resumes: Everything You Need to Know about Using Electronic Resumes to Tap Into Today's Hot Job Market by Susan Britton Whitcomb and Pat Kendall (McGraw-Hill, 2001, ISBN 0071363998, $11.95).

Expert Resumes for Managers and Executives by Wendy S. Enelow and Louise M. Kursmark (JistWorks, 2003, ISBN 1563709384, $16.95).

Top Secret Executive Resumes: What It Takes to Create the Perfect Resume for the Best Top-Level Jobs by Steven Provenzano (Thomson Delmar Learning, 2000, ISBN 1564144313, $15.99).

Writing a Résumé and Cover Letter (Barnes & Noble Basics Series) by Susan Stellin (Silver Lining Books, 2003, ISBN 0760737924, $9.95).

RECOMMENDED WEB SITES

Yahoo! HotJobs—Resume Writing:
http://hotjobs.yahoo.com/resume

ResumeEdge—Resume Writing Service:
http://hotjobs.resumeedge.com

CareerLab—Showcase your "home run" accomplishments:
http://www.careerlab.com/art_homeruns.htm

CareerLab—Cover letter library:
http://www.careerlab.com/letters

CHAPTER 7

Talking about Your Favorite Subject: You

"Have you ever worked for a green company before?"

Congratulations! Getting to the interview stage for an executive opening means you're on somebody's short list. Your application has passed early muster, and you can now consider yourself a "serious candidate" for the job.

Are you close to moving into the corner office? Well, you're closer. Let's think about it in presidential terms (which isn't entirely inappropriate, depending on the position you seek): Getting to the interview stage means you've survived the corporate version of the New Hampshire primary. You may not be the front-runner, but you're still in the race. Which means it's okay to start shopping for the celebratory champagne, but it's too soon to start icing it down. (After all, recent New Hampshire primary winners include Paul Tsongas in 1992, Pat Buchanan in 1996, and John McCain in 2000.)

Several events lie between you and ultimate election-night victory. Some are within your control; many are not. Most job seekers believe job interviews fall into the latter category. They couldn't be more wrong.

Let's continue with our presidential analogy: Election-year debates feature a variety of formats, each with their own rules, moderators, questioning methods, and the like. The diverse nature of the debates is meant to provide a level playing field for all candidates—one may be skilled in the techniques of a formal debate, while his opponent may be more adept in a town-hall format. Despite all this, in the end, each candidate exercises considerable control over the outcome. Their fortunes lie in one word: *preparation*.

Your fortunes lie in preparation as well. Yet it's amazing how many corner-office hopefuls will spend hours going over their resumes, references, and portfolios—and then walk into an interview utterly unprepared.

It's your choice: You can ad-lib your way through an interview and come off about as well as an "overly enthusiastic" Howard Dean during the 2004 Democratic primary race (with, we believe, a similar result). Or you can devote serious attention in advance to what you want to say and how you want to say it—and appear much more presidential when things heat up, as they almost certainly will.

It doesn't matter if you're interviewing at a firm across the country or within your current company: The advice found in this chapter applies equally well. In fact, internal interviews carry their own set of challenges: You may have to interview across departmental boundaries, you risk alienating coworkers competing for the same promotion, and (if you aren't selected) your search for a new position is no longer a closely guarded secret.

In this chapter, you'll discover how interviewing at this level is unlike anything you've done in the past. You'll learn what your image says about you, how to handle difficult (and perhaps uncomfortable) lines of questioning, and how to successfully navigate what may be a very lengthy interview process.

You'll learn which questions you should ask, and why you're expected to ask them. You'll recognize the methods interviewers use to exert control over the conversation, and how you can steer it back to your advantage. Most of all, you'll learn how to prepare, so that all the assets embodied in your candidacy aren't undone by momentary lapses on your part.

BEHIND THE SCENES (PRE-ELECTION)

Roughly translated, *executive-level interviewing* means "lots of questions from lots of people." You're about to face multiple interviews, over several hours, days, or weeks, depending on the whims of your prospective employer. You need to demonstrate a personality that is equal parts engaging, spontaneous, confident, and at ease no matter what the situation; a sterling character; and a determined, strategic, visionary, creative, focused mind—all to convey that you'll handle whatever pressures the job entails with grace and integrity. Here are some valuable tips:

Know Thyself

This is where those laborious hours spent with your resume pay off, and it's a major reason why we recommend that you take a very active role in writing your resume, rather than relying solely on a resume-writing service. Preparing it helps you focus on the key "talking points" of your career to date. You will become so familiar with every fact listed on your resume that discussing each item will become second nature. You'll also feel much more at ease blindly referring to it—or responding to direct questioning about it—during the interview.

For example, a few years ago, a corporate merger of two large Mid-Atlantic firms resulted in every management-level employee having to undergo interviews with the new executive team, which was trying to determine who would be offered jobs in the new company and who would be let go. David was charged with handling the technology personnel. While interviewing the IT managers, one stood out in David's mind—for the wrong reason. "He couldn't remember how a proprietary software program that he had written to handle billable accounts worked," David says. "I've never come across anyone who couldn't tell me about his own computer program."

Bottom line: Analyze every detail of your resume, and make sure you can expound on each point. You should be the best salesperson for your own talent.

Know Them, Too

Now that you know who you are, it's time to know who *they* are. You're certainly aware of the importance of due diligence; however, we can't stress enough how important it is to thoroughly research a potential employer as you prepare for an interview. They're going to be conducting a very thorough background check on you; do the same kind of check on them. The following are familiar but important steps to take as you study up on an organization:

Begin with the company's Web site. Become as familiar as possible with its history, products, geographic locations, and other details that will give you a "big picture" perspective. Many larger corporations feature an online archive of press releases. Read them. Take cues from the mission statement, but don't put too much stock in it—at the end of the day, virtually all for-profit businesses are bottom-line motivated, despite their publicly stated intentions. (Certain corporations, however, such as Ben & Jerry's, are known for being socially conscious, and you should make it your business to understand these concerns before heading into the interview.)

A great corporate Web site may also give you some insight into the culture of the company. Is it a conservative, low-risk firm? Are employees at all levels empowered to make decisions? Does it follow a standard business model, or has it established itself as an industry innovator?

One key document you should definitely try to obtain and read through before your interview is the company's latest annual report. If the company's annual report is available online, so much the better. Publicly traded companies are required to have these reports on file and provide them to the public upon request (requests are usually handled by the Investor Relations or Public Relations Department).

Trust but verify. Relying solely on a company's Web site for information is a bit like reading Soviet-era *Pravda* to get an accurate portrayal of world events. Do a little digging of your own on Yahoo! Search, in trade publications, through your personal or online network, or troll through blogs—the same sources you'd use to discover hidden job openings can also be good sources for finding "hidden" corporate details. Are the company's finances as stable as publicly perceived? What about its market share? Any rumors of imminent downsizing or other red-flag issues (internal conflicts, reorganizations, etc.) that could play a pivotal role in your ability to be successful should you be hired? Most important, which leadership qualities are most needed in the position you hope to win?

While you're tracking down data on the company, try to find out as much as you can about the people who'll be interviewing you as well. It could give you a better understanding of what they expect from a successful applicant. Do a search on Yahoo! for information on the people you are interviewing with and their managers.

If the job you're pursuing is with your current employer, your research should be significantly less difficult. The personalities and idiosyncrasies of your inter-viewers are probably well known around the office, even in large companies. Talk discreetly to trusted coworkers about who will be interviewing you. Find someone who has taken part in the hiring process with the same people who will be involved with you, and solicit their advice on what it will take for you to present yourself in the most favorable manner.

Ego Surfing

While a company can't conduct an official background check on you without your consent, there's no reason they can't learn more about you in an informal manner. If you've been published or accepted public speaking engagements in the past, information is likely available about you on the Web, accessible through a search engine like Yahoo!. While this information may be limited to little more than your name and previous writings, or a short biographical blurb related to your participation in an industry conference, other data may be available as well. Civil and criminal court filings, if unsealed, are a matter of public record, and can be obtained without your consent by anyone with Internet access.

With that in mind, it wouldn't hurt for you to discover what they can discover before the interview begins. While you're at it, speak to your references again just to assure yourself that you're comfortable with what they are prepared to say about you. Do a little "ego surfing"; find out what's available publicly about you.

Going Before the Voters

In much the same way that witnesses are prepped on their answers before appearing in court, it is critical that you be prepped before an interview. A number of questions that you'll face are predictable, and you'll be tempted to answer them without a second thought. Exercise caution, though—even with those "old standbys" you've been answering since your first job search. You want to think through your answers in advance, because the answer that appears best initially frequently isn't. On the following pages, we review some familiar interview questions, and factors to consider when answering each one.

Where do you see yourself in five years?

This question may be slowly disappearing from the standard interview. Upper-level executives often don't last five years. A survey by ExecuNet, an executive recruiting firm, found that corporate leaders remain at their companies an average of three and a half years. The name of the game is quick results, so focus your answer on what you hope to achieve in the first three to six months on the job. As long as your answer ties into the company's existing business strategy, you'll probably be able to deflect any further talk about a five-year plan.

Tell us about yourself.

This question can establish candidates as effective communicators, or expose them as ramblers with problems organizing their thoughts. Develop a thirty- to sixty-second "elevator speech" highlighting your abilities and past accomplishments, and stick to it. Think of the answer to this question as a partial biography that touches on your career in a very broad sense. Guard against a response that appears too "canned."

Less is more. This is frequently the first question asked, so keep in mind that you have numerous questions ahead that will allow you to more fully outline your personal history and character.

What is your greatest strength?

Whatever it is, craft your answer so that it meshes with some of the most sought-after leadership qualities that we discussed: vision, consensus-building, integrity, crisis management, and performance. Chapter 1 contained a list of several of these traits. Can you identify which ones are most important to your prospective employer? If so, frame your answer accordingly.

Are you creative? Couch your response in terms of vision. You want your interviewer to connect your greatest strength with one of the company's greatest needs, which is why you've taken the time to learn as much as you can about the company.

What are your weaknesses?

Everyone's got 'em, and you have yours. But there's an art to exposing them. Many weaknesses can be re-cloaked as positive behaviors: If you make snap decisions, for instance, you can "confess" to being a leader who takes action quickly, which isn't always a bad thing. Own up to it by saying that your leadership skills grew following a specific instance that, in retrospect, would have been better handled with a more cautious approach.

Why are you interested in leaving your current position? (Or: Why did you leave your last position?)

Time to put on your best diplomacy hat. Regardless of the true reason you're leaving—unbearable working conditions, unbearable boss, snubbed for promotion—now is not the time to air that particular laundry.

Spin your answer so that it dovetails with the opportunity at hand. You're not lying; in order to get this job, which you want, you need to leave your current job. This job offers opportunities for growth and new challenges, or else you wouldn't be applying for it.

Special circumstances exist if you were fired or flat-out quit. Be honest and unemotional in recounting the details. If you were fired, focus on how the experience has helped you grow in some way. If you quit, explain your actions in terms of career enhancement. Do not be evasive, because there's a very good chance that by doing so your answer will conflict with one given by a reference, and that will doom your prospects for landing this job.

Laid off? Relax. In today's economy, that's hardly the scarlet letter it once was. Focus on the skills you gained from the position.

Why should we hire you? What can you do for us?

Your answer should convince the interviewer that you are the person who best embodies what the job calls for. It should also demonstrate how hiring you would be mutually beneficial for both parties.

Example: "I understand that this company hopes to establish a stronger foothold in the widget market. I have spent the past two years helping my current employer increase its widget sales 26 percent, and I believe I can raise that figure even higher within your organization."

Don't appear desperate or overeager, although both emotions may be present. Use hard facts to present yourself as a problem solver and top performer. Remember: Your goal is to provide the interviewer with concrete evidence why hiring you is the best move for the company—a win-win for both of you.

A list of additional resources to help you prepare for the most difficult interview questions can be found at the end of this chapter (see page 109, "Recommended Books" and "Recommended Web Sites"). Now let's explore the different types of interviews you may encounter, and what to expect from each.

THE BIG EVENT

It's finally here—the date of your *first* interview. Note the emphasis on "first." Be patient: Most executive-level positions require several additional interviews before a decision is made. Why? In part because a significant amount of compensation is involved in filling a leadership slot. More important, the candidate selected could wield millions of dollars worth of influence over the future fortunes of the business. Therefore, you should be ready to wait weeks—possibly months—before learning whether the job is yours. (At the end of this section, we'll give you some tips on what to do during this corporate waiting game.)

If it's been a while since your last job interview, you may be surprised at how many different types of interviews are now the norm. As you wend your way through the process, you'll likely face a few different formats. Now that you've prepped yourself for some of the questions you'll face, it's time to prep yourself for the settings in which you'll face them.

Long-distance or Video Interviews

As much as you'd like a face-to-face meeting, it's not always possible to get one. On those occasions, technology sometimes steps in and saves the day—or ruins it, depending on how successful you are at representing yourself from afar.

A long-distance interview may be as low-tech as a conference call between you and one or more interviewers; it could be as high-tech as a closed-circuit video interview. We'll trust that at this point in your career, you've mastered how to handle yourself during a phone interview. (If not, you may want to consult the sections on job interviewing in our other job-hunting guides, *From Learning to Earning* and *Your Next Move* for a quick brush-up.)

Video interviewing is quickly gaining in popularity. On college campuses it allows employers to interview potential entry-level workers quickly and economically. At the executive level, it is used frequently when the candidate and the interviewer are on opposite sides of the country (or the globe, if you're interviewing for an international position). In addition, recruiters sometimes conduct video interviews as an initial step in the qualification process, though there are rare instances when a video interview could be part of a series of interviews between you and members of a corporate search team.

When at all possible, avoid video interviewing. All the advantages (travel savings, ability to conduct multiple interviews in a short period of time) lie with the interviewer; most of the disadvantages (no opportunity to view job site, limited personal interaction) are on your side.

If you have advance notice that you're going to undergo a video interview, try to arrange a mock video interview; many executive search firms offer such services. On the day of the interview, arrive at the site early and verify that you're comfortable with the environment: the lighting, sound, camera position, and other factors that can easily be changed to accommodate your preferences.

Behavioral Interviews

This type of interview is twofold: On the one hand, it features open-ended questioning designed to reveal your past responses to particular situations. The premise is that your earlier behavior may be an accurate predictor of how you would handle future challenges. However, these questions serve a secondary purpose: The interviewer will be looking not just at what you say, but at *how* you say it. (On occasion it's a company psychiatrist who conducts the interview and observes your behavior.) The questions reveal your ability to express yourself and to think quickly on your feet. For that reason, many questions in a behavioral interview aren't really questions at all—they're negatively worded statements that almost beg for a defensive response:

- ☼ Describe a time when you didn't achieve a goal you had set.

- ☼ Tell us about the last time you were asked to go along with something you didn't agree with, and how you handled that.

- ☼ Recall a specific moment in your current job in which you salvaged something good from a bad situation.

Because it's impossible to know in advance the questions you'll face, the best approach when preparing for a behavioral interview is to think of past failures you've had, and what you learned from those experiences—or how you achieved a positive result from a challenging situation.

For example, one of Paul's shining moments in his current position came when he and his staff opted to work a twenty-one-hour shift on the first day of a "cutover" to new technology. Paul had pleaded with his supervisors to delay the launch, because he knew the system wasn't ready for widespread rollout. However, the CEO had promised customers an early delivery date and couldn't be persuaded to change her mind.

The incident had been extremely frustrating for Paul; in fact, it was the impetus for his current job search. He vowed to use his experience in handling this event to land his next position. As a result, he was eager to respond to the question of "salvaging good from a bad situation" when it was asked.

This isn't as easy as it seems. If you're at a loss, ask the interviewer to clarify the question. Above all else, remember to remain positive both in your answer and in your demeanor. If you can find (and accentuate) the silver lining in every story, you won't be nearly as wary to discuss even the most colossal of failures. One final note: Behavioral questions aren't designed to eliminate you from contention, so don't fret too much over them. These evaluations are simply tools, and likely won't determine the final outcome of your candidacy.

Team Interviews

Despite some companies' beliefs, team interviewing does not include meeting with several interviewers in a back-to-back format. In a true team interview, you meet with several questioners at once. The major benefit here is that time isn't wasted in a seemingly endless string of interviews in which the same questions are answered repeatedly.

On the negative side, any missteps you make, no matter how slight, may not be noticed in a one-on-one setting; however, with multiple eyes on you, it's unlikely that any faux pas on your part will escape detection.

In most cases, companies are aware that a team interview can be unnerving, and they'll take steps to help put you at ease. Occasionally, though, you'll run into a bit of game playing. One of the participants may have been assigned the role of the "assassin," asking overly difficult questions and acting in a manner meant to unsettle you—the corporate version of good cop/bad cop. Don't be ruffled; in all likelihood, you're being judged on your ability to remain diplomatic and even-tempered. Similarly, be prepared to endure long periods of silence. It's an old interviewing trick meant to judge how well you react in an uncomfortable situation—and it's not a particularly effective trick, at that. The onus of keeping the conversation alive is on the interviewer, not you; if you've completely answered the previous question, resist the urge to fill the silence.

Restaurant Interviews

How can something so enjoyable as dinner be used in conjunction with something so nerve-racking as a job interview? For many people, dinner-table etiquette is a lost art. Meal interviews are popular at this level because, as an upper-level executive, you'll be expected to represent the company at social functions frequently. Being ill at ease in such a setting can derail your climb to the top.

If you're wary of finding yourself in such a situation, you're not alone. Social phobia is one of the most prevalent fears in American adults. But you can't turn

take a memo

Benefits of a Team Interview

Facing a group of people as opposed to one person can be a bit over-whelming. To effectively navigate a team interview, it helps to know the advantages such a format can provide you. Focusing on the benefits will help structure your performance.

1. As the person being interviewed, you only have to "nail" one performance. After the interview, everyone on the other side of the table will be able to evaluate your candidacy based on identical data.

2. Misunderstandings can be eliminated. Because all your interviewers sat in the session together, it will be easier for them to compare notes. If one of them is unsure about your response in a particular area, it can be cleared up quickly.

3. Call-back interviews are minimized.

4. While meeting everyone at once can be intimidating, you can turn it to your advantage. Remember everyone's name and title the first time you're introduced. During your responses, focus your gaze on whichever individual asked each question, but take care to glance at the others to gauge their reactions. If one seems to take particular notice of a reply, finish by saying something along the lines of, "Mr. Miller, I noticed that you seemed to be very inter-ested when I spoke about client retention. Would you like me to elaborate on that?"

down such an invitation and reasonably expect to survive as a candidate for the job. Brush up on the etiquette basics: which fork is placed where, which water glass is yours, and so forth. In addition, abide by these guidelines:

☼ **Follow the leader.** Don't sit until the host is seated. In fact, take all your cues from your host when it comes to alcohol, smoking, and ordering. Those are "test" areas, and your host will closely monitor your actions.

Drink only if your host does, but stop after one—even if everyone else at the table continues. Avoid smoking if at all possible, particularly if you have a tendency to chain-smoke once you begin. Try to order your dinner after your host so that you can determine which menu items would be appropriate. Above all, avoid difficult foods such as ribs, hard-shelled crabs, pasta . . . you get the picture.

☼ **Being the guest of honor is not the same as being the emcee.** Don't be the rudder that guides the dinner conversation. You need to be an active participant, but that doesn't mean you're in charge of the topics discussed. Don't be the first to open a discussion about the job you're pursuing; that's a job for your hosts to handle. If the conversation takes a turn into unfamiliar territory—let's say hunting comes up and you've never even held a rifle—simply listen *with interest* and say little. If you're asked to contribute, confess to knowing little about the subject and never make a comment that can be considered inflammatory. Now is not the time to reveal that you're an ardent PETA supporter. (However, you should *never* compromise your values. If the ethics expressed at the table offend your sensibilities, you may want to consider whether this job or company is right for you.)

☼ **Seek spousal support.** Your partner may be included in the invitation; she or he needs to be as prepared as you are. Discuss in advance the people who will be in attendance, what your expectations are, and possible questions your partner may face. You may be the one gunning for the job, but it's not unusual for companies to fret over the domestic lives of their leaders. If your spouse is uncomfortable in this role, try to subtly minimize his or her participation in the conversation.

Subordinate Interviews

During the hiring process, you may meet folks who will wind up working for you. While they may not be involved in interviewing you directly, it's possible that their impressions of you will play a role in the final decision on whether or not you get the job.

Who are these people? Anyone you meet with a direct tie to the company. They run the gamut from midlevel manager to office assistant to company driver. Just by coming into contact with you, they're in a position to offer a comment about you. Your task: Convince them that, if asked, you're someone they'd want as a leader.

QUESTIONS YOU SHOULD (AND SHOULDN'T) ASK

Interviews are dialogues, not inquiries. Yes, you are the star attraction, and most questions are directed toward you. But remember: You're also expected to pose some questions of your own.

However, you can't simply dive headlong into a cross-examination. Like everything else we've discussed in this chapter, there's an art to handling this aspect of the interview.

Rule #1: Never, Ever Bring Up Salary

There is a proper time for talking about your compensation package, and that time isn't now. You're seeking an executive-level position; odds are that the money and benefits tied to it will be substantial and extremely negotiable. While it may be tough to shake the "What's in it for me?" mentality that has been a benchmark of previous job interviews, resist the urge to focus on the financial rewards you may reap in the position you're pursuing. You're a big-picture employee now; if you're the one they want, they'll take care of you.

A time will come—*after* they've determined that you're the right person for the job—when compensation becomes a primary topic. (We deal with that, in detail, in the following chapter.) It is *not* a topic for the interview process, and it's your job to make sure that it doesn't become one. If the subject is broached, graciously deflect the question:

Q: "What type of package are you seeking?"

A: "If it's determined that I'm the person best qualified for the job, I trust that we'll be able to reach an agreement that is mutually beneficial for both of us."

Rule #2: Get a Realistic Lay of the Land

Adopt a secret agent's mind-set as you head into the interview process: Be persistent in ferreting out the company's top secrets. If problems exist—problems you'd be expected to solve—you should be told about them during the interview process. Demand this information, because whoever wins the position will be expected to produce some tangible results quickly, and these results may include drastic changes. Find out what the expectations are, because it will help you determine if the job is a good fit for you.

Most companies will be surprisingly forthcoming about the current state of internal affairs, because they'll usually require corner-office candidates to sign confidentiality agreements. In fact, more often than not, nondisclosure agreements

(NDAs) are required to even begin the interview process. NDAs may prohibit you from communicating anything you learn during your discussions to anyone else; likewise, you can't indirectly profit from any knowledge you gain. If you believe you're being stonewalled, remind your interviewers that you are bound by the agreement and insist on being provided with as much information as possible. Who knows? Your tenacity in this area may just be another test to see how you react under pressure. In any case, you deserve a complete accounting of how things currently stand—and how things should stand once you come on board. Any organization unwilling to share details with you (such as its financial reports or sources of funding) is probably one best avoided.

Rule #3: Show Them What You Know

Ask questions that demonstrate your knowledge of the company and its mission. This is a golden opportunity for you to show your interest in taking a leadership role in the company; the worst sin you can commit is to passively answer questions and offer nothing in return. During your preinterview research, you should have uncovered financial statements and other data that, when reviewed, brought questions to your mind. Are there problems inherent in the company's business model? Is a major organizational shakeup on the horizon—and, if so, how would it affect your department? Be careful, however: Avoid questions that would embarrass those conducting the interview. It's probably not necessary for you to know the answers to those kinds of questions, and you'll only create an adversary when it comes time for the vote on whether to hire you.

take a memo

Ask for the Sale

One CEO we spoke to, who has interviewed many executives in her career, shared a unique interviewing strategy with us: When the interview is complete, she stands up with her hand extended and says, "Thank you for your time." If the candidate doesn't "ask for the sale" (inquire as to when they will speak in the future) she will not hire him, no matter how well he interviewed.

What Your Appearance Says about You

Even entry-level interviewers are well versed in the basics of appearance, so we're not going to waste your time on that here. However, there are considerations unique to job-hunting at this level.

If you're a "more experienced" worker, you may be concerned about competing against younger applicants. Although you can't change your age, you can change the *perception* of your age. If you're worried that the job calls for a more youthful appearance, take appropriate steps: Exercise, change your hairstyle, adopt an enthusiastic persona. While you're at it, take a look at your wardrobe: Does it fit the corporate culture of your potential new employer?

During the interview, pay careful attention to the essentials: body language, eye contact, and facial expression. Develop a confident, relaxed smile; it will pay big dividends during moments when, internally, you're a cauldron of anxiety. Most of all, stay alert and engaging at all times.

Additionally, be aware of your mannerisms and speech. You're striving to become a corporate leader, which means your public image may need some polishing. If you have videotapes of your public speaking engagements, watch them with a critical eye. Could you express yourself better? Do you have any gestures or motor tendencies (such as frequently running your fingers through your hair or clicking your pen) that should be reined in?

Post-election: Follow-up

Finishing up a round of interviews (or even a single, strenuous one) should leave you with a sense of accomplishment. You've done everything possible to win the position, and now you're left with little to do but wait—which, as we've previously mentioned, can be a lengthy process on its own.

Ah, but there's still more work to be done. Your postinterview actions could be as vital to your success as those taken before and during the interview. Despite how it may feel to you, this isn't "downtime" by any means: Your merits are being measured against those of other candidates. A little additional nudge from you may be all it takes to put your name above the others.

Give Thanks

Thank-you notes (or follow-up letters) are mandatory; send them to everyone involved in the interview process, including the executive recruiter. Make it a point to collect business cards from each individual with whom you came in contact. When writing thank-you notes, don't worry about giving the appearance that you're subordinating yourself to people who may report to you. There are plenty of ways to "write around" that issue. If they were active interview partici- pants, they should receive a note from you.

Several resources are available to help you craft the perfect letter. Remember: A thank-you note serves as a quick reminder to decision makers that you're interested in the vacancy, and also allows you to . . .

Provide Clarifying Information

Despite your best intentions, interviews sometimes hit an awkward moment. You may have had a difficult time describing how your current responsibilities have prepared you for a leadership role. Perhaps those conducting the interview didn't get a clear sense of a certain segment of your skill set. As you replay the events of the interview process in your mind, you may recall a moment you'd like to revisit. In your thank-you note, you could offer to clear up any fuzziness, but *only* if you're sure it exists; otherwise, you may be highlighting something negative that wasn't noticed by others in the first place. Unless you sincerely feel the need to revisit an interview moment, you're better off by simply offering to answer any follow-up questions.

MOVING ON

You may be the perfect fit for the organization; you may have nailed every inter- view perfectly. Yet you may not get the job, for numerous reasons. Corporations frequently promote from within, or they may want someone with a stronger background in marketing, team-building, budgeting, etc. After sending all your follow-up letters and thank-you notes, allow yourself one final phone call to gauge whether you're still viewed as a viable candidate for the position.

Think strategically: Should you call the recruiter, a hiring manager, or the primary decision maker? You can't call all of them without seeming obnoxious, overly anxious, or both. Determine which person is likely to give you a clear-cut idea of where things stand in the firm's executive search, and contact her. One caveat: Wait one week after sending your follow-up letters before making this call. Once the call is finished, begin planning your next search. You may yet receive an offer, but focusing on your next steps will prevent you from dwelling on an unchangeable past and help you chart your future course.

If the job you sought was internal, the ball is completely out of your court. You either won the job or you didn't; if you did, they'll tell you, and if you didn't, well, they'll tell you that also, *as soon as they are able to.* Good companies keep their employees "in the loop." This is especially true for those on the executive career track. You've done everything you can to win the promotion; don't sabotage your future efforts for advancement by showcasing your anxiety or impatience.

After all, those traits *don't* appear in our list of leadership qualities.

RECOMMENDED BOOKS

101 Great Answers to the Toughest Interview Questions by Ron Fry (Thomson Delmar Learning, 2000, ISBN 156414464X, $11.99).

201 Best Questions to Ask on Your Interview by John Kador (McGraw-Hill, 2002, ISBN 0071387730, $12.95).

The $100,000+ Job Interview by Wendy S. Enelow (Impact Publications, 2005, ISBN 1570232229, $19.95).

Fearless Interviewing: How to Win the Job by Communicating With Confidence by Marky Stein (McGraw-Hill, 2003, ISBN 0071408843, $12.95).

How to Interview Like a Top MBA: Job Winning Strategies from Career Counselors, Recruiters, and Fortune 100 Executives by Shel Leanne (McGraw-Hill, 2003, ISBN 007141827X, $12.95).

Landing the Job You Want: How to Have the Best Job Interview of Your Life by William C. Byham and Debra Pickett (Crown, 1999, ISBN 0609804081, $14.00).

RECOMMENDED WEB SITES

Yahoo! HotJobs Career Tools—Interviewing:
http://hotjobs.yahoo.com/interview

BestKnows—During the Interview:
http://en.mimi.hu/career/during_interview.html

Yahoo! Finance—Company financial info and press coverage:
http://finance.yahoo.com

How to Interview:
http://www.howtointerview.com

The Professional Image—Article and Interview Archive:
http://www.theprofessionalimage.net/press.html

CHAPTER 8

Payday: Negotiating Your Compensation Package

"Hi, Ted. Love your latest salary."

Well, congratulations should be in order right about now! For any of the following information to be useful, you must have received an offer. Your job search is over at last, assuming you and your new employer can reach an agreement on the compensation package.

Therein lies the rub. Navigating salary talks at this level likely will be more complex than any contract negotiations you've engaged in up to this point. Today there are a myriad of ways in which employers can choose to reward their leaders. Many won't show up in your paycheck, but are just as valuable as cash— sometimes even more so because they're tax-exempt.

The good news at this point is that you and your employer can enjoy a bit of a "honeymoon" period. Both sides are enthusiastic about the new alliance and eager to forge ahead. This isn't a war, after all; there are no losers at this stage, and, importantly, *at no point in the pending discussions should either party feel like one*.

In this chapter, we'll discuss the art of negotiation, the types of compensation available to you, steps to take to ensure that you're getting the best possible deal, and how to structure your severance package in the event that you and your new employer part ways in the future. Follow the blueprint contained in these pages, and we're confident that you'll strike a much better deal for yourself.

EVERYTHING IS NEGOTIABLE

Our advice throughout this book has been to avoid the topic of compensation through all previous stages of the hiring process. Here is where it pays off, and why.

Think of contract negotiations in terms of a high-stakes poker game. If you've successfully fended off questions about your current salary up to this point, you're like the player who's held his cards close to the vest. Others at the table (in this case, those who've made the decision to hire you) have an idea how strong your hand is based on the "up" cards—the details they're already privy to.

However, the more "down" cards you have, the more speculative they're forced to be when it comes to what you already have, and the initial offer will tend to be somewhat higher because of this. (Note that we don't suggest bluffing about your current compensation package. If you're discovered, it could negatively impact your relationship with the employer and you'll be viewed as lacking integrity. Even if no one calls your bluff, it could weaken the nonadversarial relationship you're trying to establish during these discussions.)

take a memo

What the Executive Recruiter Knows

Of course, at this level, some of the players—the executive recruiter, for example—already may be aware of your present compensation. That's vital information for the recruiter to have up front, because it helps in the initial search; there's no sense forwarding you as a candidate unless the position offers substantial pay and/or career enhancement.

Beyond that, it's not necessary for the recruiter to know much more about your personal life. In chapter 3, we cautioned against getting too "chummy" with a recruiter, especially if the company retained the recruiter to conduct a search that ultimately netted you. In that situation, the recruiter becomes (by extension) a part of the corporate hiring machinery, and as such should be viewed as another player on the other side of the negotiating table. At best, you can view this kind of recruiter as a neutral party at the table. However, in general, the recruiter's client is the *company*, and that's where his allegiance lies.

But no matter how many cards have been shown, please understand this: There's always room for negotiation. Whatever the market conditions, whatever the economy, whatever they already know about your current package, there's always wiggle room.

Even though you're probably looking at a heady salary figure, plus bonuses and benefits you've only dreamed of previously, there's more room for negotiation at this level than at any other level at which you've been employed. This kind of flexibility may not be in the area of salary; then again, there's a good chance you've already found the salary to your liking. We're talking about senior-management positions, after all, and an attractive salary is the easiest thing your new employer can offer.

If this is your first foray into the upper echelons of corporate America, you may be stunned at what's available. Perquisites, or "perks," have long been a staple used to entice (and retain) people in executive offices. While many of these perks have come under scrutiny from increasingly irritated (and embarrassed) shareholders, there are still plenty of attractive—and legal—offerings to be had. However, before you can determine what to negotiate for, you must first understand the different types of compensation available to you at this level.

TYPES OF COMPENSATION

When it comes to executive-level compensation, American companies are (finally, some would say) entering the age of oversight and accountability.

Recently, exorbitant severance packages have sparked public outcry on several occasions. Here is a sampling of recent news stories illustrating how executives' parting perks have gained national attention:

July 15, 2005

UNDER FIRE, RETIREMENT SYSTEM CHIEF TO RESIGN

RICHMOND, Va. (AP)—The chairman of the Virginia Retirement System said he will heed Gov. Mark R. Warner's demand and resign amid revelations he crafted a sweetheart exit package for his predecessor. Alfonso I. Samper, the Warner-appointed chairman of the VRS, crafted the $263,000 exit package for W. Forrest Matthews Jr. The General Assembly's investigative arm, the Joint Legislative Audit and Review Commission, criticized the severance as unauthorized, excessive and cloaked in secrecy. Matthews had headed VRS for only three years when the board told him last fall his dismissal was imminent. In December, Samper concluded a deal with Matthews worth two years' pay at Matthews' annual salary of $131,000.

—Norfolk Virginian-Pilot

July 12, 2005

DEPARTING MORGAN EXEC TAKES HOME $32 MILLION FOR SHORT STINT

Loyalty is a prized commodity on Wall Street, and in the case of Stephen S. Crawford of Morgan Stanley, it has paid a $32 million dividend. Mr. Crawford's pay package is particularly unusual because he was co-president for only three months, yet he will take home a severance package that pays him as if he had been co-president for two years and allows his stock to vest—the executive-suite equivalent of hitting the lottery.

—Landon Thomas, Jr., New York Times

Does all this mean that the salaries and benefits of corner-office denizens are finally being reined in, just as you begin your rise to the top? Not at all. Corporations continue to reward their executives handsomely, a trend that shows no signs of abating. If anything, it's accelerating. According to a 2005 report released by United for a Fair Economy and the Institute for Policy Studies, today's CEO, on average, earns more than 400 times the salary of an average worker. Just two decades ago, it was a 42-to-1 ratio, which didn't raise the hue and cry—in the press and among shareholders—that today's lofty executive salaries have.

The heightened awareness of the disparity between executive compensation and the average worker's paycheck has had an impact: Firms are becoming ever more innovative in how they reward their leaders. Your benefits in the past may have included only the basics: health care, a dental/vision package, a 401(k) option, and a company pension plan. These will obviously continue to be components of your compensation.

However, executives also enjoy numerous additional privileges not available to other employees—everything from country club memberships to personal use of the corporate jet. Because these benefits typically fall outside the boundaries of shareholder or legislative review, board compensation committees are turning to these perks to sweeten their offers. According to a 2005 special report by *Forbes*, the average Fortune 500 CEO received more than $10 million in compensation in 2004. Only about 20 percent came in paycheck form, and—perhaps as a result of increasingly negative publicity combined with new accounting rules making it a less attractive option to the employer—compensation via stock options dropped to about 33 percent.

Because you'll be negotiating much more than a straight salary, you'll want to retain the services of a good lawyer or compensation specialist as you go forward (we'll talk more about that later in the chapter). They're essential if you hope to get everything you deserve, and if you hope to understand the total package once you get it. Your task right now is to become more familiar with some of the "standard" benefits executives receive—you'll want to have at least a passing knowledge about these matters yourself.

In the next few pages, we'll discuss the most common components of a compensation package at this level—and what each one may mean for you.

▶**Action Item: Think Big: Your Wish List of Perks**
Before reading further, list five perks you would like to receive once you're in a corner-office position. After reading this chapter, revisit this list. Are there any items that you'd like to modify or replace?

1. _____

2. _____

3. _____

4. _____

5. _____

Base Salary

By now, you should have a very good idea what someone in your position makes, whether within your company or with a competitor. Several factors affect this figure—geography, job experience, and company size, just to name a few—but it pays (literally) to know what the job is worth, so that you can determine two dollar amounts: what you want, and what you will accept. Your starting salary should fall somewhere between those two figures.

Don't have a ballpark idea of what the job should pay? You haven't been doing your due diligence. If (as described in chapter 3) an executive recruiter contacted you about the job, she should have given you a general idea of the compensation to expect. You also should have researched the salary for similar titles within the industry and within your region, and for someone of your experience, while you were preparing for the interview process back in chapter 7. In any event, you *must* arm yourself in advance with this knowledge if you hope to gain the best possible package.

Bonuses

Bonuses are meant to enhance your base salary; they can be awarded for corporate performance, meeting strategic goals, or other reasons. Many companies favor bonuses over higher salaries for their top leaders because this gives them the ability to tie pay to performance; for that reason, you'll want a contract that clearly spells out your bonus plans and what is required for each bonus to kick in.

While most bonuses are meant to be part of your overall pay, *signing bonuses* are used to boost a candidate's initial offer. They allow the company to increase your pay while at the same time pacifying alarmists on the executive board (or in the accounting department) who may feel uncomfortable recommending a lofty starting salary. It goes without saying (although we'll say it anyway) that the signing bonus is a one-shot deal; you can't go back the following year and ask to receive it again. For that reason, you may find it helpful to set it aside when contemplating your offer and focus only on the items (salary, other bonuses, and benefits) that will come up for renewal each year.

Stock Options

This is not the same as getting stock straight out, which may already be part of your package; stock options could be a very profitable (or completely useless) benefit because of the conditions tied to them.

Shares of stock received directly are yours to keep; there may be a vesting date (the earliest date at which you can sell) tied to them, but you could hold them forever if you chose to do so and the company remained solvent. Stock options, on the other hand, are stocks that you have the option to purchase at a previously agreed-upon price before the option expires. The price of the option (called the "grant price") will typically be fair market value. You may be given a Notice of Grant. This is a document that details the terms of your options, including the number of shares, purchase price, and the expiration date. Read it carefully.

You'll need to wait until a certain date before you can exercise your options, and you can expect other dates to be locked out as well (for example, near the end of your company's fiscal calendar as well as near or on scheduled dividend-award dates). When you decide to exercise an option, you "purchase" shares at that point (at your grant price) and then sell them at whatever the market price happens to be.

This can be an extremely lucrative benefit, as long as the stock has risen and you have a significant number of options. Do the math:

Let's say you have an option on twenty thousand shares (at $14.50 per share) that expires after five years. Four years later, the company stock is trading at $36 and you've elected to cash in. You "pay" $290,000 (20,000 shares x $14.50), but you sell for $720,000 (20,000 x $36). Your profit (not taking tax into consideration) is $430,000—and you never spent a dime.

Of course, stock options are worthless if the stock price falls, which is what happened to thousands of "paper millionaires" during the dot-com bust a few years back. For that reason, your overall compensation package should not rely too heavily on stock options.

Many companies are cutting back on offering stock options in the aftermath of new accounting rules that treat options as expenses. Gone are the days when companies could create compensation for their top executives out of thin air, which is basically what stock options could do (at least within profitable companies). The backlash over executive pay has increased accountability. At the same time, the popularity of restricted stock grants (discussed in the next section) is rising. One final note: Given your lofty position within the company, you may be blocked from trading if you are considered an insider or have material nonpublic information about the company. Be sure to review your company's Insider Trading Policy.

Restricted Stocks

This form of compensation is becoming more popular and has even begun trickling down the corporate ladder to lower-level employees. The appeal of restricted stocks is that you, as the recipient, assume no risk. Restricted stocks are shares in the company that are given or awarded to you; sometimes these stocks come with a performance or profitability clause tied to them, meaning that you can only cash them in once you reach certain specified performance or profitability targets. In any case, unlike stock options, the current (or future) price of restricted stocks is irrelevant to you. You win no matter what.

Let's say you receive 2,500 shares of restricted stock when its price is $30 a share. You own, therefore, $75,000 worth of company stock. The stock will have restrictions on when you can sell—some of it may vest each year for the next three to five years, or it's possible that the whole package may require at least five years before it becomes nonforfeitable. Unlike stock options, you don't need to take any action when the vesting date arrives, although the value of the shares is then considered taxable income. You can own the stock indefinitely. In our example, let's assume that your company has fallen on hard times, and the stock is down to $11 a share. You can sell your 2,500 shares and pocket $27,500 (again, not taking taxes into consideration).

401(k) Plans

Most employees take part in 401(k) retirement plans, but government regulations limit their usefulness in your case. Still, it's a good idea to participate to the fullest extent possible, because every dollar you put into a 401(k) is untaxed until distributed.

The 401(k) limit rises slightly each year, and setting aside $14,000 to $15,000 of your annual salary (plus an additional $5,000 for those over age fifty in 2006 and $500 more annually) for retirement is great for most employees; however, many highly compensated executives, including (hopefully) you, may find this ceiling exceptionally restrictive. For that reason, many executives also augment their retirement savings with a supplemental executive retirement plan, or SERP.

Supplemental Executive Retirement Plans (SERPs)

The Employee Retirement Income Security Act, known as ERISA, limits the amount of money an employee can contribute, and thus receive, from most company pension plans. These restrictions are set high enough so that they typically don't affect the rank-and-file; however, highly compensated executives may find that ERISA-qualified plans don't provide enough retirement income for them to maintain their standard of living. Supplemental pension plans exist for just this reason.

Minimal federal rules are placed on supplemental pension plans; each company crafts its own supplemental plan, hoping to placate (and attract) high-earning executive talent. Because ERISA contribution limits don't apply to supplemental plans, neither does the tax-deferral that ERISA-qualified plans enjoy.

One type of supplemental pension is the Supplemental Executive Retirement Plan, or SERP. These plans have two key features: They are intended specifically for upper-echelon workers; and they typically do not require an employee contribution. Corporate 401(k) plans (and other pension plans, as we'll see) are subject to governmental regulations that cap their effectiveness for high-earning employees, so companies turn to SERPs to make up the difference. Your SERP's value will depend on whatever formula the company uses; the company's goal is to help its executives retire to a lifestyle to which they are accustomed.

While SERPs can be worth several hundred thousand or even millions of dollars, there is one major drawback: Unlike 401(k) and other ERISA-qualified plans, SERPs are not protected by any governmental regulations. They can be eliminated if your company goes through bankruptcy proceedings, because your relationship to the company is viewed as that of a creditor. Still, when you consider the limitations inherent in 401(k) and company pension plans, a SERP may be a benefit worth requesting.

Executive Insurance Plans

Executive insurance plans (EIPs) can benefit both the company and you as one of its executives. As policyholder and beneficiary, the company protects itself from loss in the event that you (as an integral employee) happen to, well, die. These plans sometimes provide your employer with cash to recruit your successor. However, EIPs can also be structured to provide your family with enhanced retirement income and/or death benefits. Unlike SERPs, executive insurance plans aren't affected by bankruptcy proceedings, which make them an attractive benefit to acquire.

Deferred Compensation

How much money do you really need to live comfortably? If the answer is, "A lot less than what they're willing to pay me," then deferred compensation may be a benefit worth exploring.

The definition of *deferred* compensation is pretty straightforward: You postpone receiving some (or all) of your salary and/or bonus payments until some point in the future, such as when you retire. The benefit to you is that you pay no taxes on the money until you receive it. Your company benefits because the money that would have been paid to you stays in its bank account.

Just as with SERPs, however, you risk losing your deferred compensation if the firm goes belly-up. For that reason, accept deferred compensation only if you can truly afford to do so—and if you truly believe in the long-term viability of your company.

Severance Packages

If you think of all the benefits noted above as various cuts of beef from the cash cow you hope your job will become, then your severance package provides the juice that creates the sizzle. Severance deals—otherwise known as "golden parachutes"—have drawn the lion's share of scrutiny in the executive compensation arena. Accordingly, we've devoted an entire section at the end of this chapter to this issue.

Miscellaneous Perks

It's nearly impossible to create a comprehensive list of executive-level benefits, because companies are exceptionally willing to consider almost any reasonable request imaginable. This isn't to say that you'll have carte blanche to structure a sweetheart deal for yourself. Shareholders and other employees serve as somewhat effective watchdogs against exorbitant practices at many (but not all) large firms.

Still, it seems as though there's almost no limit to the potential perks available. Consider this partial list of fairly common additional benefits your new corner-office position could offer:

- ☼ Short- or long-term housing allowances
- ☼ A pied-à-terre (temporary or secondary place of lodging)
- ☼ Relocation expenses
- ☼ A company car (or car and driver)
- ☼ Travel expenses
- ☼ Extended leaves of absence
- ☼ Educational expenses
- ☼ Club memberships
- ☼ Vacation residences
- ☼ Private facilities for bath/exercise
- ☼ Low-interest (or no-interest) loans
- ☼ An executive dining area and/or personal chef
- ☼ Use of corporate jets
- ☼ Tax reimbursements
- ☼ Financial planning/estate planning services

Realistically, if you're making your first foray into the world of executive leadership, many of these benefits may not be available to you—yet. But knowing what's out there—if not now, then in the future—sure helps kick-start your new, longer workday, doesn't it?

PREPARING FOR NEGOTIATIONS

First step: Get a lawyer, and one familiar with executive pay issues. Better still, find a compensation consultant. Every barber needs a barber, and even Doogie Howser needed a doctor when he got sick. You may be a great deal broker; maybe your skills helped you land your new job. However, no matter how confident you are in your negotiating abilities, trying to chart your own course here will be difficult and is best left to experts who can devote their full attention to this issue. You'll be busy enough getting acclimated to the suddenly lofty expectations thrust upon you.

Some executives find their compensation falls into a 20–80 format: 20 percent of what they earn is in direct cash (salary and cash bonuses), with the remaining 80 percent coming in the form of benefits. Whether or not this applies in your case will depend a great deal on your salary and any bonuses

take a memo

Enlist the Aid of Experts

A **compensation consultant** or **pay coach** is your personal concierge as you progress through the stages of your journey toward the corner office. Your consultant can research the salaries and benefits typical for the position offered, offer you advice on how to handle questions during the deal-making process, help you hone your negotiation skills, and even play "devil's advocate" during mock salary discussions to help you feel more comfortable when the real thing takes place. There is great peace of mind in turning over the worries of discovering what you're worth (and what your future job should be worth) to an expert.

The bad news: This assistance doesn't come cheap. Consultants charge hundreds of dollars an hour, and the cost is borne solely by you.

The good news: Because you're footing the bill, your compensation consultant works for you—unlike a recruiter, who usually has ties to your prospective employer or must remain neutral at best.

The best news: In many cases, a first-rate compensation expert will actually put money in your pocket, because he can help you craft a package you may only dream of being able to win for yourself. For most pay consultants, the majority of their business comes from working directly with companies to establish appropriate compensation packages for the company's employees. Therefore, these consultants have a wealth of knowledge as to what's standard and what's possible. If you can afford to spend a few thousand dollars on one, consider it a good investment in your future earnings.

that are realistically obtainable. Again, as we mentioned a few pages earlier, your research on what the position should pay will give you a clear idea of the salary you can expect. Assume, for the moment, that you'll receive it. What next?

For starters, create a spreadsheet in which you establish a monetary value for every perk you seek. This isn't a buffet; you're not trying to see how much you can heap on your plate during one visit to the dinner bar. Instead, you're determining the relative worth (to you) of the benefits you'll possibly receive.

In many cases, this isn't too difficult: If you receive x amount of stock (or stock options), and you anticipate that it will be worth y dollars by its vesting date, simply multiply x by y to calculate the value. (One note of caution: When it comes to evaluating the future worth of corporate stock, studies have shown that employees—not the company—tend to overestimate. Also, don't forget to account for taxes when determining what you will receive.)

However, when it comes to other perks (such as club memberships), the monetary worth may not be equivalent to the price you'd pay. Country club memberships, for example, don't mean much if you don't use the facilities.

On your spreadsheet, include a justification for each benefit. You may be asked to explain the necessity of certain perks, and having an answer ready will certainly help your cause.

For example, when Daniel relocated from Florida to a technology firm in the Northeast, he didn't want to leave his thirty-two-foot fishing boat behind. The boat represented a substantial financial investment he had made just two years earlier. He asked his new employer to foot the bill for transporting the boat northward. By researching the costs associated with such a move in advance, Daniel allayed any misgivings his new boss may have had about such a perk; his request was granted.

One last point, as you prepare to negotiate: Conventional wisdom holds that the first side to submit a figure in any negotiation immediately becomes the weaker party at the table. However, there are two factors to keep in mind: First, if you've postponed discussing compensation until this point in the process, then the first reference to a specific salary should come with the offer of employment. Second, the reality is that the compensation you're seeking is not entirely a mystery; either your executive recruiter knows what you make, the employer has a general idea of what someone in your current position earns, or you submitted a salary history. And, of course, your salary is already known *to the penny* if you're moving up at your current place of work.

In any event, the idea that the first side to mention a figure loses ground is so ingrained in American workers' minds that the services of a compensation consultant are justified. It will help eliminate any lingering feelings of paranoia that you "blinked first" during the process. Working with a compensation consultant will give you greater confidence overall as you go through the negotiating process, and it may make that process go more smoothly and quickly.

THANKS, BUT HOW 'BOUT SOME MORE

Okay, things are really moving now. With or without a salary consultant's help, you've received an initial offer, and it's lucrative. Attractive though the initial offer may be, you need to have it sweetened—even a little bit. Accepting the first offer could weaken your negotiating stance in the future. It could make you look more passive than you'd like to be perceived. In any event, it's advisable to be gracious when the offer is made and then request time to review it before responding.

You may not need a dramatic improvement, and that's one of the advantages of executive-level positions. There are plenty of areas where you can improve the deal, even slightly. So turn it down—but do it with an eye toward showcasing your business and diplomatic acumen:

> **Good:** *"I have problems with this offer that I'd like for you to address."* You're getting your point across, and that's a start. But you're also putting the burden of remedying the situation entirely on the other side, and that's not the best strategy.
>
> **Better:** *"I appreciate the offer, but I'd like to discuss some of the specifics with you."* Very artful. You've expressed gratitude, dissatisfaction, and team-building—all in one carefully crafted sentence, and without making the other side feel defensive about their position.

As you ask for more, remember that—to the company, at least—the offer is already fairly lavish. Their search for you took weeks (more likely, months), not to mention many thousands of dollars. Nobody is about to "go cheap" on you at this point.

When you turn down the initial offer, do so tactfully, lest you risk offending someone involved in the talks. That person could be a factor in your future, and any hard feelings you foster could come back to haunt you. When heads start rolling in dire economic times, yours may be first in line if you aren't the top producer and your posturing during salary negotiations sparked a bit of ill will. This is particularly true if you are among the highest-paid executives in the company.

Call it the "ticket-taker law of accountability": On an interstate highway, almost all of us are guilty of speeding. We're all trying to get ahead, because getting ahead is best for us. When you stumble onto a speed trap, you're probably fine if you're moving with the flow of traffic and not being obvious about getting ahead. If, however, you're driving noticeably faster and more aggressively than those around you, you're the unfortunate soul who gets pulled over.

Surprisingly, many people who are adept at negotiating complex contracts for third parties find it difficult to do so for themselves. Others may be used to putting team goals ahead of their own. That's why, as we mentioned earlier,

take a memo

The Five Be's of Negotiation

Here are five surefire negotiation strategies:

Be knowledgeable. If you're already well compensated and receiving a variety of benefits, you may not have as good a grasp as you think on your current earnings. Remember that spreadsheet you created to evaluate the worth of benefits being offered? Do the same for your current position, so you can do a line-by-line comparison of what you have now versus what you're being offered. The Yahoo! HotJobs salary calculator is a good place to start. Simply enter details such as your years of experience, your industry, and your location, and the calculator will come up with the salary range you can expect to earn.

Be realistic. Your employer's ability to provide compensation will depend on many factors, such as company size, financial capabilities, short- and long-term strategies, and your skills and experience. If you know your talents are in a high-demand field, you'll be able to nudge the offer higher; if, however, you believe that the job could just as easily be filled by someone else, tread lightly when requesting that the offer be amended.

Be ready to give when you take. Negotiation goes two ways, and you'll find that something you want that normally would be considered "off the table" isn't so difficult to acquire if something else is removed in its place. For example, if you won't need educational reimbursement, mention that you'd be willing to forgo that option in order to enhance your relocation benefits. It helps, again, to be specific about your request: "My children are in grades eight and ten, and moving them in the middle of the school year would be a real hardship. I'd like to have my family remain in our current home until July."

Be diplomatic. As talks continue, maintain a cool and pleasant demeanor. It will pay big dividends once you're in the job. If, by chance, talks fall apart and you're never able to reach an agreement, send a letter of thanks for the offer and express hope that you can work together in the future. You never know.

Be aware. Pay careful attention to their responses to each request. Are they acting fiscally responsible, or are they trying to skimp on your salary offer at all costs? If it's the latter, you need to ask yourself if you believe that you'll receive the proper funding and support to be successful. If you don't, rethink whether you really want the job after all.

using a compensation consultant is such a good idea. Don't assume that your compensation consultant will negotiate for you; in fact, most of these consultants remain behind the scenes, and with good reason. Your employer may cast a wary eye on the entry of an outside party into salary discussions.

ONCE THE DEAL HAS BEEN STRUCK

Very little is left to do now except to get to work. However, there are a few common-sense guidelines you should always follow at this point:

1. **Get everything in writing.** In a best-case scenario, every offer and counter-offer will have been made in writing, because this provides a record that all parties can follow throughout the process. The final offer definitely needs to be in writing, and on corporate letterhead. This won't be a problem—the written offer gives as much protection to the employer as it does to you. The only problem that could possibly crop up is if you lose the document. So don't lose it.

2. **Don't go back for seconds or thirds.** By this we mean that once you've reached an agreement, stick to it. Remember: Integrity and honesty are two of the most highly sought-after leadership qualities. Trying to revisit your con-tract after the fact will harm your reputation in those areas. No matter what you've suddenly "remembered" that you need or would like added to your compensation—continued care for an aging parent, for example—it's best just to kick yourself quietly for forgetting it in the first place. You'll return to the bargaining table soon enough, typically within a year or two. Save any additional requests for that point in the future, and move on for now.

3. **Turn down any counteroffers from your current employer.** We hate to be sticklers on that integrity thing, but accepting a counteroffer from your cur-rent employer—no matter how attractive—may damage your reputation and your career in ways that compensation can never make up for. At the very least, you may never be able to consider any future offers from your would-be employer, because you may never get one. Additionally, you could risk word getting around within the industry that you're a person who doesn't honor your agreements. Last, you could return to a work environment where hard feelings are festering just below the surface. You were willing to leave the first time; your supervisors and your coworkers may wonder when you'll leave the next time around. Oh, and when times get rough and belts get tightened, guess who'll be among the first invited to leave?

Hello, I Must Be Going

Your severance package needs to be negotiated at the same time as the rest of your compensation; however, because it plays such a large role in many executive pay packages, we've chosen to deal with it separately.

As mentioned previously, these exit benefits are attracting the ire of American workers and shareholders, as well as the attention of federal regulators. For that reason, corporations are becoming a bit more skittish (and conservative) when doling them out. This isn't true at the highest levels, however; CEOs and other top leaders are still collecting golden parachutes with outrageous provisions. If you're not entering the "inner circle" of the corporation, you can assume that your agreement will be somewhat less extravagant. Still, it's possible to fashion a deal that serves your interests very well in the event of your departure.

What should you seek? The tempting answer is, "Whatever you can get," but that may be a bit too simplistic. You should approach your severance agreement the same way you approached the other portions of your compensation. First, create a list of what you'd like to win during the discussions. Second, specify why each item on your wish list is essential. Finally, be willing to engage in some give-and-take during the bargaining process to get the items that are most important to you.

Companies may have guidelines they follow in their severance agreements, but every employee's situation is unique. Benefits that would cost a significant amount of money for you to provide for yourself, such as medical coverage, are not a burdensome cost for your employer to bear. Your company may be surprisingly willing to meet your demands, particularly if it helps to avoid problems in the event you and the company end up parting ways. With that in mind, here's a list of some details your severance agreement could include:

Severance Pay

This is by far the most important aspect of your parachute package. Many companies utilize a formula (such as one month's salary for every year of service) to determine the amount of severance pay.

Strive for an additional amount if you're going to be working much higher on the corporate totem pole. Remind your employer that you have no intention of leaving the company or performing at a mediocre level, but that you'll feel more comfortable knowing that additional money is there in case unforeseen circumstances arise.

Stock Grants

This has the potential to be a contentious area, especially if your future departure happens to ruffle a few feathers (think back to the examples of egregious departure perks mentioned earlier in this chapter). Stocks can be granted upon your exit, or your agreement could specify that any unvested stocks (or options) already held by you can immediately vest as you leave. In either case, using stocks as severance compensation can have a significant impact on how much you walk away with.

Continuing Medical Coverage

If your company has more than twenty employees, federal law requires that you be offered the opportunity to receive continuing medical benefits for a limited period, at your cost, when you leave. It's possible to talk your employer into footing the bill for this coverage for a specified length of time. It's one less expense to worry about as you search for your next job.

Noncompete Agreements

Here's a severance item that is *never* in your favor. *Don't sign a noncompete agreement without first having your lawyer approve it.* These clauses, which prohibit you from seeking employment with a competitor for a specified period after you leave the company, have the potential to bring your next job search to its knees.

Noncompetes do offer one slightly ironic advantage; the existence of a noncompete might actually strengthen your argument for additional severance pay and benefits, because a very restrictive NCA could render you virtually unemployable for a lengthy period of time.

Reason for Leaving

Carefully review the wording that deals with the particulars of your departure; are any benefits no longer applicable if you're terminated "for cause"? If so, it would be in your best interest to have "for cause" spelled out in your employment contract. Does this stipulation include poor sales, a sinking stock price, loss of market share, or any other factors that may not be within your control?

Your agreement should also work in your favor in case you don't lose your job "for cause." You should not be penalized for opting for retirement (or early retirement), for a decision to switch careers, in the event of a corporate reorganization or a merger with another entity, or other reasons that have nothing to do with your performance. All those could be viable reasons to leave.

At this point you should feel fairly confident: You have an attractive compensation package and are ready to take on greater responsibilities, either at a new company or within the upper ranks of your current organization. In the next chapter, we'll discuss ways to begin your new job on the right foot and avoid common pitfalls.

Recommended Books

Executive Compensation Answer Book (Aspen Law & Business, 2002, ISBN 0735532206, $145.00).

Get Paid What You're Worth: The Expert Negotiators' Guide to Salary and Compensation by Robin L. Pinkley and Gregory B. Northcraft (St. Martin's Press, 2003, ISBN 031230269X, $13.95).

In the Company of Owners: The Truth About Stock Options (And Why Every Employee Should Have Them) by Joseph Blasi, Aaron Bernstein, and Douglas Kruse (Perseus, 2003, ISBN 0465007007, $27.50).

Negotiating Your Salary: How to Make $1,000 a Minute by Jack Chapman (Ten Speed Press, 2001, ISBN 1580083102, $12.95).

Responsible Executive Compensation for a New Era of Accountability by Peter T. Chingos (John Wiley & Sons, 2004, ISBN 0471474312, $70.00).

A Woman's Guide to Successful Negotiating: How to Convince, Collaborate, & Create Your Way to Agreement by Lee E. Miller and Jessica Miller (McGraw-Hill, 2002, ISBN 0071389156, $16.95).

Recommended Web Sites

Yahoo! HotJobs—Salary calculator:
http://hotjobs.yahoo.com/salary

Salary.com—Salary and compensation articles:
http://www.salary.com

Society for Human Resource Management—Offers a compensation and benefits forum:
http://www.shrm.org/hrlinks

Bureau of Labor Statistics—Features useful facts and trends:
http://www.bls.gov

Severance FAQ—Sponsored by the Executive Law Group:
http://www.severancefaq.com

ExecPay Inc.—Compensation consulting firm:
http://www.stockcompensation.com

Hr-Guide.com—List of compensation consultants:
http://www.hr-guide.com/data/048.htm

Inc.com—Includes articles on benefits and compensation:
http://www.inc.com

Executive Pay Study from United for a Fair Economy and Institute for Policy Studies:
http://www.faireconomy.org/press/2005/EE2005_pr.html

Forbes.com—Special Report on Employee Compensation:
http://www.forbes.com/2005/04/20/05ceoland.html

CHAPTER **9**

The First 100:
Hit the Ground Running

"It's Monday morning, Miss Berstresser. Let the merriment commence."

Welcome to the corner office! You've impressed the company's leadership, negotiated a fair compensation package, and are ready to assume your place at the top. What happens now?

Short answer: A whole lot, and rather quickly. Taking a leadership position—whether you're leading an entire company or a department within a large firm—can be overwhelming, particularly for those who've never before stood on this lofty rung of the corporate ladder.

Every situation is unique, but what leadership positions all have in common is this: Whatever situation you've been thrust into, you were needed. You were selected. And you are responsible for your team's success (or failure) from this point on.

Full accountability is the biggest responsibility of executive leadership. During the dot-com start-up craze in the late '90s, many companies reshaped their business models, flattening layers of bureaucracy under the guise of sharing decision making among a broader base of employees. In many cases, this "bubble management" business model meant that the classic supervisor/employee distinction was blurred. Employees could work on a variety of products and services, reporting to any of a handful of project managers and department supervisors. In some cases, it worked; however, in others it led to growing confusion and frustration over who was in charge of making which important decisions—and who should carry out those decisions. Despite efforts to appear innovative, the theory of shared responsibility and minimal hierarchy rarely works for the following reason: At some point, someone has to make the hard decisions. Starting today, that person is you.

Like many books of its type, this book has guided you through the job-search process: from finding the hidden job market to working with executive recruiters, strengthening your resume (and your list of references), preparing for interviews, getting the offer, and navigating salary negotiations. Unlike other books, however, we aren't going to leave you there. The "What next?" question is just as important as all the other questions we've answered so far. With that in mind, it's time to determine what your next move (or, more precisely, moves) should be.

EARLY EXPECTATIONS

When incoming presidents take office, reporters make quite a fuss over the "first one hundred days" of the new administration. Whether or not such scrutiny is fair is arguable; trying to alter the course of the federal government at times must seem like using oars to turn an aircraft carrier around. But constituents—even those who didn't vote for the winner—want results, and sooner is always better than later.

If the leader of the free world must face early expectations, it's fair to assume that you should too. Go into your new position knowing this, and use the time leading up to your on-the-job debut—the period between when you're hired and when you start—to plan some early successes.

Don't gun for earthshaking changes, unless the situation you're entering is so dire that nothing short of an all-out revolution will do. Even then, small accomplishments are fine—in fact, they'll probably seem larger than they really are, simply because your tenure as the new leader is in its "honeymoon" phase.

George W. Bush's first one hundred days as president in 2001 were fairly nondescript. Nothing of true substance occurred in that period, with one exception: Expectations of White House personnel were clearly spelled out. Bush insisted that staffers dress professionally, even when working on weekends. He was also a stickler for on-time attendance at meetings. Those decisions had little to do with the job of running a nation, but they did instill the feeling that change was coming. Roger Wilkins, a professor of history at George Washington University, summed it up during a 2001 appearance on CNN's Newshour with Jim Lehrer by saying, "They look grown-up, as opposed to the prior group."

Examine the sidebar on "Presidential Beginnings" on page 134. Interestingly, the presidents judged to have had the most effective starts to their administrations entered office in times of significant crisis: FDR inherited the Great Depression, Johnson had to contend with the assassination of a popular predecessor and a growing war in Vietnam, and Reagan faced high unemployment and a national malaise.

There's a lesson here. Do you see it? You may be stepping into a dismal situation where bold strokes are needed quickly, and you have to establish your authority right away. If so, you should have been briefed on the "state of the Union" during the interview process, giving you time to formulate an effective plan of attack.

Of course, the opposite may be true. You may be walking into a positive situation. Perhaps the previous leader postponed retirement until a smooth transition was assured, or the company is coming off multiple quarters of solid performance. Shareholders, employees, and your superiors are happy, and you haven't even reported for work yet!

Avoid the temptation to become complacent—your first moves are *still* being watched, and your leadership ability is *still* being evaluated. You need to consider the direction the executive board and other senior-level executives are headed,

take a memo

Presidential Beginnings

Wondering how to spend those first few months in your new office? Here's a look at the first one hundred days of various twentieth-century presidents, along with each one's approval rating for the "First 100." (Note that the presidents' approval ratings upon *leaving* office often changed dramatically from these early results. A leader's accomplishments and legacy—whether he is leading a country or a corporation—can only be assessed over the course of time.)

Franklin D. Roosevelt: Sent numerous bills to Congress that were enacted quickly and formed the basis for his "New Deal" administration; these moves eventually helped pull the nation out of the Great Depression. While poll numbers are not available for Roosevelt's first one hundred days, it is not difficult to imagine that the results would have been favorable. (The Gallup organization did not begin collecting survey data until 1937, which coincided with the beginning of Roosevelt's second term.) Most observers credit his "do something now" mentality with spawning the "100-day" presidential benchmark.

John F. Kennedy: Approved the Bay of Pigs military action in Cuba, which had disastrous results. (However, Kennedy's popularity helped him enjoy robust approval ratings throughout his shortened presidency.) *"First 100" approval rating: 77 percent (Gallup).*

Lyndon B. Johnson: Pushed for (and won) congressional approval for the landmark Civil Rights Act of 1964. *"First 100" approval rating: 78 percent (Gallup).*

Ronald Reagan: Quickly slashed government spending and won approval for tax cuts to jump-start a floundering economy. *"First 100" approval rating: 68 percent (Gallup).*

Bill Clinton: Launched an ambitious (but controversial) health-care initiative championed by his wife; instituted a "Don't ask, don't tell" policy on gays in the military; and reversed himself on a promised middle-class tax cut. *"First 100" approval rating: 45 percent (CNN/USA Today).*

and where they'd like you to steer the course. A good situation simply affords you the luxury of taking your time before instituting major changes, but there remains much to accomplish. Although you're not being asked to reinvent the wheel, you are expected to make it roll more smoothly than it did before. As rosy as things may be, there's plenty of anxiety regarding your entry into the picture.

Regardless of which set of circumstances you encounter, planning your actions beforehand will help optimize your chances for success and minimize inadvertent gaffes and missteps as you approach your first day in the corner office.

ENGINEER YOUR ENTRANCE

Your new job begins the moment you accept it, regardless of any lag time between when you're hired and when you actually start working in your new position. Yes, you have some endgame responsibilities to take care of in your former job, and, yes, you should leave on the best of terms, whenever possible. The "Don't burn your bridges" mantra always rings true. However, don't let the job you're leaving behind negatively impact the job that lies ahead.

One of your first considerations should be how your hiring will be announced, particularly internally. Assume that your staff members will be given the heads-up before word reaches the public. If it appears that this isn't happening, ask why and insist on correcting the oversight. No one likes to find out who her new boss is through a press release or a news item in the business section of the local paper.

You also may want to consider an informal question-and-answer session with employees well in advance of your start date. Remember: The mere fact that someone new is in charge is enough to create tension and anxiety in many workers, particularly if you're stepping into the shoes of someone who had been well respected.

This is a great opportunity to spell out, in general terms, your strategy for the group. You can explain what you're hoping to accomplish in a specified period (say, the next two quarters), how you'd like to see those goals achieved, and what reaching for those goals might mean for the people working with you. However, be aware that going the Q&A route may be dicey, especially if you're entering a panicky environment. Your hiring, taken by itself, may be construed as a signal of significant changes ahead—not the most welcome development in many companies, especially those that have been resistant to change or have recently faced a great deal of negative change.

From the Desk of

Anil Arora, CEO, Yodlee, Inc.

My experience in the business world has consistently led me to the conclusion that success is a combination of two things: (1) building business, and (2) building people. Building business is 30 percent strategy and 70 percent execution. Strategy is about an objective, fact-based under-standing of the marketplace, competitors, and what can create a sustainable competitive advantage. Execution is about passion, insights, attention to detail, and innovation.

Building people is all about cultivating leadership, account-ability, ownership, talent, chemistry, and fun.

Industry experience is overrated; the fundamentals are the same. If you follow the above principles, you will get the results that will lead to the corner office. Think of your career as a marathon, not a sprint! Think about learning, growth, and results rather than titles and money. Most of all, if you do some-thing because you like it, you're good at it, and you genuinely enjoy it, you'll be a success.

Yodlee, Inc. is the pioneer of "account aggregation" powering online financial applications for millions of consumers worldwide.

Your primary goals should be to reassure those reporting to you and win them over to your vision. Project and instill confidence that the situation is about to change for the better, and do your best to convert any nonbelievers as quickly as possible.

Answer all questions they have honestly; keep in mind that integrity is very high on the list of sought-after leadership traits. But it's okay to be vague if the conversation enters a high-anxiety area, such as the prospect of layoffs or a salary freeze:

☼ Good: *"I am confident that most of our cost-cutting will come through normal staff attrition and perhaps a shifting of existing resources."* In other words, a loss of jobs is imminent, but hopefully the company won't be resorting to mass layoffs—though that is still possible.

☼ Better: *"We are looking to cut costs, and I'd welcome your suggestions about ways to do this without causing undue hardship. Please feel free to e-mail me any ideas you have along these lines."* You may be committed to downsizing, and you haven't dismissed that possibility with this statement. You have, however, offered hope that you are receptive to avoiding this step if an attractive alternative is proposed. First impressions (both good and bad) are lasting ones. That's why engineering your entrance is such a critical opening step.

BUILD YOUR TEAM

Your days of ensconcing yourself inside the comfortable confines of a team are over. That doesn't mean you can't surround yourself with talented people. It just means that you're the lightning rod for the team. As such, you should exert as much control as possible (in other words, as much as your superiors will allow) in shaping that team.

A new U.S. president begins naming Cabinet members weeks before taking office. During this period, a transition team puts together recommendations for appointments, timelines for policy initiatives, and plans for implementing both sweeping and incremental changes. In a similar fashion, you need to assemble your inner circle in advance of, or soon after, taking over. Diplomacy is required; in most cases, the positions are already filled. If you haven't had a chance to interview the current leaders among your staff, now is the time to do so. You'll discover some you can't wait to replace and others you may want to hang onto.

If your plan all along has been to make across-the-board personnel changes, or if you have specific people in mind to take over certain positions, you should have addressed these points during your job interviews. Unless you're at the CEO level, someone—the board of directors or the president of the company—has ultimate authority over your hiring decisions. You're better off knowing in advance that your wishes will be granted.

WIN THEIR HEARTS AND MINDS

Whether you've entered a good or a bad situation doesn't really matter once you're installed as the new leader. You'll have your share of naysayers and critics, no matter what the circumstances, and you should be extremely surprised if you don't. The idea of small successes is worth repeating: Plan to accomplish something, and then accomplish it. These achievements will be building blocks for more important successes down the road. More important, you'll win converts over to your side.

This is where "eating the elephant" comes into play. The answer to the well-known riddle "How do you eat an elephant?" offers sound advice. Take things one bite at a time, and celebrate the fact that it's one less bite to worry about as you move forward. Eat the elephant by grappling with individual problems rather than groups of problems. Here are some of the benefits of this approach:

- ☼ It will help you get a better grasp of your staff's capabilities.

- ☼ Results, however small, will occur more quickly.

- ☼ Employees will tackle a single problem more eagerly than a lengthy to-do list of items that need attention.

Adopt a positive attitude to achieve your goals, even if it goes against your "taskmaster" nature. Remember: You're in the early stages of elephant-eating; negative reinforcement will cause your employees to focus on the size of the beast that remains to be eaten instead of the forkfuls they've already consumed.

Be generous in your praise for accomplishments, no matter how small they are. Be cautious in your criticism over setbacks, and never criticize publicly. If you must reprimand someone, do it in private and as diplomatically as possible (try offering an alternative solution), and follow up to ensure eventual success.

As your success rate grows, you will find it easier to increase the demands you place on your employees. They will see that not only do you have a plan in place, but it's actually working. The elephant is growing smaller. Success not only breeds more success, it breeds believers—and a team full of believers will help you perpetuate the cycle of success.

IF YOU'RE NOT PART OF THE SOLUTION . . .

While he was vice president at Gannett New Media, Phil Fuhrer had this axiom for all employees: "Don't come to me with a problem unless you're bringing me the solution at the same time."

What a great time-saver! Some employees (you probably know a few) thrive in "crisis du jour" mode; it's almost as if their sense of workplace importance derives from identifying problems—over and over and over again. Effective leaders already know that problems exist. Focus your efforts (and those of the people around you) on solutions. By requiring that solutions accompany the announcement of a problem, you can eliminate unnecessary distractions in the workplace while at the same time ensuring that your staff has a head start on resolving any real issues that crop up.

LEADERSHIP GAFFES

As we've mentioned, even the best leaders make mistakes, and there are two schools of thought when it comes to them. The first: Do everything you can to eliminate virtually all mistakes. The second: Mistakes are how we learn, from infancy through adulthood.

You can certainly subscribe to both theories at the same time. In your first one hundred days, however, it's advisable to opt for the former approach rather than the latter. Again, this is why planning is so crucial; in fact, the same

Korn/Ferry International survey, mentioned on page 138, found that the failure to establish priorities was the most common mistake senior executives made in their new positions.

Other mistakes on the Korn/Ferry list included:

☼ Committing cultural or political errors. A closed-door meeting of top Texaco executives (all-white) in 1994 was secretly taped, leading to a successful $176 million class-action lawsuit when at least two of them were overheard referring to African-Americans as "black jelly beans."

☼ Waiting too long to bring about change.

☼ Spending too little time with subordinates.

☼ Shying away from difficult personnel decisions.

We'd like to add a few to this list. In particular:

☼ Thinking that you have all the answers. Nobody does. If you did, you wouldn't need to surround yourself with a top-notch executive team, because you could orchestrate everything in Wizard-of-Oz fashion from behind a massive curtain.

☼ Acting too quickly. It's sometimes as costly as not acting at all. Recognize the dynamics of the situation you are entering, consult with others (your team and the people to whom you report), and avoid "knee-jerk" reactions that you might be taking just for the sake of "doing something."

☼ Getting rid of all the dissidents. You'll have a very skewed perception of reality if the only people you talk to are sycophants. You need rebels. You need someone around who isn't afraid to reveal that the emperor has no clothes.

That said, the best advice is probably this: Try to avoid mistakes, but don't be averse to making them. Executives who never make mistakes rarely figure out how to fix them.

On Your Way

One final thought, as you plunge forward into your new leadership role: Your first executive position likely will not be your last. Make your mark. If, having done that, you discover that your position will last a lifetime, savor your extraordinary good fortune. If not, remember that most leadership positions last less than five years—and virtually all leaders move up in their careers.

take a memo

CEOs Speak

The Boston Consulting Group (BCG) published an eye-opening article in 2002, titled "Assuming Leadership: The First 100 Days." The authors asked twenty CEOs to evaluate their first months in office and come up with agenda items they would follow if they could begin their jobs anew. Here is a sampling of responses:

- ☼ Assess the company's leaders and make necessary changes within thirty days.
- ☼ Clearly communicate goals and make sure employees understand how you will achieve them.
- ☼ Meet with ten salespeople on the front line and with ten major customers. Such meetings provide different perspectives on the business and what can be done to make it more successful.
- ☼ Pay attention to your personal habits, including how early you arrive for work, how you allocate your time, and how thoroughly you prepare for meetings. A leader's every move is scrutinized by those around her.
- ☼ Learn how to "manage upward." When communicating with the board of directors, set realistic expectations and clearly explain goals and risks.

You've worked hard to get to where you are, and you deserve to enjoy the fruits of your labor. But avoid growing stagnant. Continue to grow professionally and evaluate where you are as opposed to where you want to be. If you've made it this far, you should feel confident that you have much to offer any organization. Never stop striving for professional fulfillment. And if the view from your corner office turns out to be less tantalizing than you expected (or becomes obstructed by a taller, more modern building filled with alluring new career opportunities), we hope that you'll use the advice in this book to move on to an even more satisfying position.

Good luck!

RECOMMENDED BOOKS

The Dynamics of Taking Charge by John J. Gabarro (Harvard Business School Press, 1987, ISBN 0875841376, $35.00).

Equipping 101: What Every Leader Needs to Know by John C. Maxwell (Thomas Nelson, 2003, ISBN 0785263527, $9.99).

Leadership 101: What Every Leader Needs to Know by John C. Maxwell (Thomas Nelson, 2002, ISBN 0785264191, $9.99).

Right From the Start: Taking Charge in a New Leadership Role by Dan Ciampa and Michael Watkins (Harvard Business School Press, 2005, ISBN 1591397928, $12.95).

Taking Charge in Your New Leadership Role by Michael Watkins (Harvard Business School Publishing, 2001, ISBN 1578516595, $34.95).

You're in Charge—Now What? The 8-Point Plan by Thomas J. Neff and James M. Citrin (Crown Business, 2005, ISBN 1400048656, $25.00).

RECOMMENDED WEB SITES

CIO—A Survival Guide for New Leaders:
http://www.cio.com/archive/120103/hs_management.html

The Boston Consulting Group:
http://www.thebostonconsultinggroup.com

INDEX

ARTIST CREDITS
for Chapter Openers

Chapter 1: Joseph Farris
Chapter 2: Frank Cotham
Chapter 3: Robert Mankoff
Chapter 4: Carol Cable
Chapter 5: Ed Fisher
Chapter 6: David Sipress
Chapter 7: Mick Stevens
Chapter 8: Robert Weber
Chapter 9: Jack Ziegler